Poetry of Aloha

"The Fire of Love"

A ke Ahi A ke Aloha

Poetry of Aloha

STEPHEN CARBON

Autumn Rose

The cascade of luminous smile enchants the trees as
stars fade, Sunlight crests above the horizon.
A morning fog of hazy mist hangs low upon the corn.
Meandering above the meadows in wispy clouds you can
touch and almost walk upon the fluffy white of nine.

In stillness of the sunrise... nature's soul begins to awake.
Her effervescent beauty in vibrant colors, petals of silk,
irresistible of my touch. I am her creation, she is mine.
From birth to death we share the Makai of blue, the Mauka to the
heavens. An earthly paradise we share of aloha, the oxygen of life.
My senses intoxicated by your eloquence, simplicity of
nature saturate my flesh and heartbeat against me.

I see my reflection in her eyes and try to envision hers looking
back into my soul. Does she sense my emotions of aloha thick as the
passion of my existence for her touch of intimacy and romance?
We walk among the mist of innocence and fate. Passion and
pain of separation to feel the reality of touch and caress.

Her petals of Autumn drip of dew upon my cheek as
we kiss before the heat of light can dry them.
Nature's tears of aloha bid goodbye to the stars of our night.
A lingering fragrance of pua in the air awakes my memory of her poetic heart.
Sunrise with my Autumn Rose.

Prisms

The passion of the stars holds no boundaries of time and space.
Eons ago we met along moonlit waterfalls of silk and lace.
To one day meet again to rekindle hearts of kind.
Unwritten chapters to fill a poets mind.
Fields of tarot dreams and romance to find.

The one who stirs the constellations of direction.
To follow starry skies and dreams of conception.
Once again we find each other's company in warmth of affection.
For however long may it be in this lifetime.
Cherish the divinity of souls of attraction.
A hui hou my island pua.

A friendship of aloha is beyond horizons yet to be found.
Where the prisms of the sun kiss the sea.
Clouds of cumulus disappear into the mist of the makai.
Opulence of earth and sky meet dreams of humanity.
The reflections and brilliance of nature's creation weave the fabric of life.
Gentle reminders of faith beyond our horizons.
To touch the softness of early evening stars in the warmth of another hand.
Eyes of blue meet darkness of hers on the caress of waves.
Islands and worlds apart but a dream shared by my wandering poetic heart.

My Hawaiian Lullaby

When trade winds blow
through green fronds
A night breeze sings its
enchanting song
Rustle and sway... gently
leaning palms
Cast in moonlit silhouette
Sea of Polynesian stars
Creations divine internet
Her touch mystify
My Hawaiian lullaby

Hair draped long in dark velvet
Tassels in wind brushing bronze
shoulders... alluring and exquisite
Fragrant voice lilting notes..
calm my beating chest
Soothing waves against my jagged cliffs
Warmth of full moon tide
My Hawaiian lullaby

Her eyes reach out to me
Gently stirring...incessantly yearning
Tidal surge and rainbows arc
Singing poems of distant meadowlark
Melt away my wintry blue
Sacred beach of Maha'ulepu

We sit among the lava
rocks and wild pua
Lost Eden in dewdrop mist
Plumeria tucked behind left ear
filters through hungry lungs
Awaken slumbering
passions like rising sun

She knows her power of
illuminant might
Touch upon my mortality of life
Infinite wisdom... divine spiritualist
Sails in my journey of consciousness
Reverberate echoes of waves
soothing my jaggedness

Tidepools gather the seas
treasures beneath my feet
Staring up into the milky way
I wander across time... wet like
warm sands of concrete
Destiny of humanity in
bronze sculptures solidify
Her fragrant smile
My Hawaiian lullaby

Set in stone.. buried in time capsules
Her earthen soil holds the
richness of seed of creation
Nurture my elements of
carbon with tears of aloha
Touch upon fronds in
peaceful winds of Konu

The divinity of her compassion
fills the air tonight
Choirs of angelic stars in
oceans of moonlight
She lives forever upon lyrical sky
My Hawaiian lullaby

Song of Peace

A wish upon the stars my darling as you rest your
beautiful eyes and heart of passion
To chase your dreams of romance
Along a path of iridescent prisms
Follow your heart and you will find sanctuary of great fortune
A song of peace within to enchant your warmth of soul
Somewhere over rainbows I await your wandering poetic heart
Across seas of tidal moons you are in my thoughts
We walk among the cherry blossoms as light rain falls
A soothing breeze through the trees
I hold you tightly in my mind as you drift off into starlet dreams.
Will you dance with me under the stars my darling?
My princess of Hawaiian beauty
May we touch the softness of rainbows in our eyes
Feel the sensuality of you against me in the moonlight
My enchanting girl of mystery lay your soft essence
of desire against me as you sleep tonight.
Starlight streams in dream laden clouds amongst the stars.
Moonrise above calm sea bless in sparkle into watery eyes.
Warmth of trades through palms filter with fragrance
of your aloha... the touch of a lei never lost.
Northern star rises in distant constellations.
Shimmering lanterns from a poets thought once read.
Until the morning sun crests may her heart rest in slumbering tides.
Awake to new found inner strength and desolate peace of locked passions.
A new day to greet distant horizons.
May the lei of Hawaiian blessing touch my island pua with aloha.

Everything Happens for a Reason

Wild pua and peppermint
Like the daffodils of spring chasing winters lament
The arc of double rainbows of summer season
The autumn leaves crisp upon shimmering frost
The whales of winter migration
Everything happens for a reason

The solitude of empty hearts smashed upon the cliffs
The resentment of stinging tendrils of saltiness
Washed away withered inside
My words can only foment the pain of ones soul
Cut by rigid corals of the rip tide
Everything happens for a reason

May shepherds of the sea be your guide in nurturing notions
Across distant lands and dark depths of oceans
Find your serenity of passion in sun dried sands
My northern star on lost horizon
Cast a light of friendship
To my enchanted island
Everything happens for a reason

Mine is a voice in the trades of distant dreams
A quill in the ink of meandering streams
Carrying forth a melody of morning sun beams
Touch upon your cheek in soft kiss most serene
Warmth of aloha to you my darling of destiny
Everything happens for a reason

Driftwood

Dreams are in your grasp as the stars cast their light
A mind adrift in the conscious of soul
Swept along by the churning tide of emotions
To discover the intimacy of distant shadows of moon
Glisten like morning dew upon island pua strewn
Cool salt air waft across warmth of white sands and bronze shoulders

Twisted spindles... sun bleached archives of the sea
Fathoms of iridescent beauty, lost treasures of history
Sacred totems of mystery and awakening
Wave driven contours, limbs coalescing
Feminine curves of dexterity, enchanting spell of sensuality
Shelter our hearts... ghostly tridents, white remnants of Kanaloa

Wash upon new shores of destiny stone branches of island tapestry
Driftwood scatters in poetic sculptures, statuettes of turquoise isle
Glancing forth in reflective contemplation our soulful allure
Lyrics to transcend and permeate the pulse of consciousness
Timeless in wait beneath yellow orb and coconut mist
May your heart find its beat serene
Next to the one of your dreams

Me ke aloha Pumehana

Star Rise

The oceans salt dries upon tidal rock as light fades
Memory of auburn hair tassels in cool trades
Bronze her tone, Hazel eyes radiant
Depth of song within
A resonant sound from distant shore

Reflections of evening light
Enchanting melody my northern star of the night
Across the darkening sea she rises to greet me upon the waves.
Calm...her inviting heart
Warm ocean smiles and reflects her sparkle

Cresting waves lyrical in nature find the perfect
rhythm as our horizons disappear
Earth and sky blend together darken
Starlit the hemisphere
High above to paint her artistry upon my eyes of blue
Lyrical charm intrigues my soul of worn shoe

Radiance of late day sun against my flesh as evening palms cool
Warmth of the stars to fill my heart
within my grasp or forever apart
To touch the aloha of a friends greeting
Across the mist of the makai
A crescent moon rises
Silhouette of Polynesian cliffs
A new spirit arises
A lyrical melody attracts
My northern star of distant light
Dance with me into the night

Wandering Souls

My mind wanders in thought this eve. I hope you have a moment to listen...

I sometimes wonder how the sands of eternity feel beneath ones feet. The warmth of a gentle tide against ones flesh and blood. Is it possible our dreams are the bridge we cross every night but only halfway to this labyrinth of heavenly shores. To face our virtues of humanity only to be turned away and returned to this world.

Would we recognize ourselves beyond the mirrors in our life. Our family, our friends. I find myself in a shallow tide of blue my darling swirling around my feet as the granules wash past my toes. The earthly blue around me. Feeling it wash out beneath my weight of existence. To reveal all that I am and have given to this world. I stand in soulless wonder at myself.

How does my life carry out its purpose when witnessing the demise and dust of another living being. Related through the same life blood of aloha to witness and travel this world of poetic landscape. For such a short time we have on this beautiful island in the galaxy of stars. A mystery I behold and bequeath unto my sister's humble spirit.

A destiny of aloha I seek in the spirit in my footsteps. We should recognize the rarity of two souls who share a vision of life as one and to cherish it. Protect its sovereignty and nourish it when it is suffering. We will never fully understand the realms of our reality and dreams but follow in its light of guidance and draw strength and fortitude from its warmth of melody.

My thoughts may seem scattered across the stars of Maha'ulepu but the warmth of island sand is still felt beneath.

Tide Pools

The music of our life brings me
to our special place of passion.

Multitude of waves to have caressed
Maha'ulepu beach over eons of time
wash over me in tidepools of aloha.
A solitude of souls ingrained into the
cliffs hold her secrets of dreams. The
sweetest voice of passion beckons my
presence and impressions upon her lips.

The fire of Pele in her soul burns bright
for her Knight to return. The essence of
lost love teases my mind in eagerness.
Somehow.. I know this lady of poetic
passion. As familiar as the lyrics of
a favorite melody her heart sings
out in desire. The magic of two souls
blossoming into a romance never seen
before permeates the island breeze.

The sweet taste of honeysuckle upon
your neck stirs deep into my senses.
Unforgettable your scent of pua in
my embrace my ku'uipo. The feel
of your flesh and heartbeat against
me I so miss this eve as I stare up at
the stars and moon. I wish our eyes
gaze up into the same night sky.

Traversing the galaxy of time our
shooting stars collide in fervor of

poetic justice. The life of the universe
combines in the elements of carbon
to create our star child of dreams.
A solitude of souls we will always
share as my heart sings out in joy
tonight. I hope you hear the sound
of my voice missing you my island
pua in the Koloa air tonight.

I drift into the night sky
Along moonbeams of an island song
Lyrics of aloha flow in leeward tide
Precious exuberance sing out
Nurtured young hearts of starlight
Seasons illuminate the soul
Almond eyes of blue
search the horizons
Sundress flows flippantly
Tossed by trades
Focus of dream laden rainbows
Balanced in step a
Frost upon her heart
Never to be forgot
Miles apart
Melt like glaciers
Misty Makai of blue
Wash the Nihiha shells along her shores
Sacred hearts of treasures
Revealed in receding tide pools
Touch to my soul of aloha
Forever in poetic passion
Impressions of my heart

Lei of Aloha

Lei of aloha lay upon me
Blossoms of orchid, plumeria, maile and ti leaves woven in Lei of sacred hands
Lay upon me in effervescent light
Fabric of memory on this cold winter night

Rapture of fragrant emotion in island rain forest
Feathery petals of Hawaiian pua
Silk impressions upon my chest.. aloha touch and subtle caress

Starburst colors of mother nature radiant in sunlight
Lei upon my yearning soul
Delicate flower of life
Breathe in your essence of aromatic spice

Wash away my rigid pulse of darkness in showers of lunar shades
Fluttering butterflies
Mingle in gentle trades
Pollinate our nectar across island fields in early sunrise
Lei of aloha never dies

Forever adorned with eternal
spirit of life
Her touch induce me... alluring beauty
Opal eyes invite
Smile of colors... vibrant and bright
Waltz upon white sands in softening daylight

Lei of creative design
Bless me with touch of Hula soul
Celestial hips move like constellations across space and time
Wrapped in poetic verse
Submersed in planetary realm
Saturate my flesh and dreams
Free my prison of dark fathoms of seas
Release my passion and intimacy
Infinite waves of energy

Lei of aloha
Lay upon me

Plumeria Petals

I was walking in a garden of plumeria along the sea
I dreamt of her...
A silhouette of a girl in the distance
Standing alone in shadowy cliffs...meditative thought
White Plumeria petal perched behind left ear
Hair flowing in trades... warmth of sunlight reflecting Hawaiian tan
Drawing steps closer she looks, smiles a beguiling wink
Almond eyes meet for a moment
Star of Venus in evening sky
Energies blend with a radiance of orangey sunset.. heat of lava
Tropical scent of plumeria in the breeze
Garden of serenity and passion
Lips of glistening dew beckon my touch of masculine attraction
A friendship of hearts once imagined
Like wild Naupaka growing along sea cliffs
Two souls clinging to earthly soil
Sustenance of life together we embrace the emerging
constellations of seventh heavens
Flowers of island paradise
Essence of hula dance and reverberating heart beat
Lay upon me with silky softness of the evening breeze
We share the beauty of Neptune's stars in a moment of earthly dream
Souls attract like lost lovers past eons of longing memory
Poetic thoughts unveil life's mystery
Seeds of fertile creation interweave dreamscapes and fantasy
Brought to consciousness
Where dolphins dance across the universe
A melody of song find their magic in lyrical verse
Depth of emotion to fill deep ocean Discovery of
truth within and aloha of devotion

Vines of Naupaka

The sun looks to shine upon hearts of courage
A peaceful illuminance on wildflower fields
Crepuscular rays through cumulus clouds of nine
Vines grow thick and intertwined.. her earthly sign most divine
A soulful yearning sings a melody of mind

Oceans of light... her oxygen of life fills the air as I surface
Like whales inhale the first breath from the sea with a burst
I shimmer and splash upon her oceans of white caps and waves
Dive deep within her fathoms of undersea caves
Soulful eyes reflect the mirror of emotion locked away
Apart by tides and seas of sunlight
Distant allure her culture of Polynesia delight
Destined to dance with her essence in gray moonlight

Tarot dreams and passions of lace
Forever revolve around each other in a celestial embrace
Discover new energies as magnetic fields attract
Like the sun and earth flower interact

A poetic verse of natural elements
Converge in resonance and loving kiss
Softness like the petals of tulips
Grace my cheek and fingertips
I hold you in my dreams and try to feel your touch of honeysuckle lips
Stars of Jupiter await in passionate seeds of reunion
When hot embers ignite in sunlight of summer season
Follow your courage of heart and mind of reason
To create new life and music in artful merge of freedom

Lost Eden

Looking west across emerald sea
Fertility of divine plumeria seed
Petals of white golden dreams against undulating waves of sunbeams
Almond eyes with skies of Hawaiian blue
Warmth of charm, radiant and true
Sparkle like diamond stardust
Heavenly gift are you
Breathe in her fragrance of Polynesia...aromatic pua
Sparks ignite and embolden my view
A wisp of gentle romance
Envelope my senses, forces familiar
Lyrics interlope the stars
A moonlit melody in songs eternal
We dance upon sands of time and destiny
Hearts unfold upon chapters of fate untold
Ancient scrolls of souls discovered
Unravel our chaotic journey
We only seek the peace of happiness in each other's shadow and life energy
Compelling flow of aloha preordained
Effortless..
Natural forces of gravity
Impossible to resist... magnetic essence
Inebriant as wildflower in morning mist
Grace my cheek... full soft breathy lips
In dreams of aloha your touch and caress saturates silken flesh
Intimate thoughts I must confess
A passion to share amongst the heat of sun
Lay upon earthen petals of yellow hibiscus
Create bonds of carbon in distant island bliss
In a nebulous of aloha
A seedling grows in rainforests of Magdalene gardens
A divinity of attraction... spirituality
Her immaculate touch of lost Eden... my sacred mystery

Lucid Dreams

The stars bend into prisms of rainbows… strum my melody for a girl I humbly
adore. Shimmering down upon my eyes of blue makai. A heart filled with peace,
joy and vivacious energy pours forth a sweet fragrance of far eastern spirit.
My musical soul feels her sensual touch. A baptism of my
soul. A silent lucidity. A blessing of friendship within.
Her presence forever imprinted in my heart and soul. Polynesian dreams grace
her melody of friendship and aloha, impressions upon sands of distant ocean.
The mist of lilikoi fills my lungs. My thoughts hold onto her lingering kiss.
The earthly paradise we share, lyrical meanings of expression, form bonds of the
elements of life…unite us on this journey of planetary existence and beyond.
We slow waltz to ignite the embers lost amongst the stars of Kauai
Celebrate the cherished blessings of friendship and aloha.
To begin anew with heart songs painted across pastel
sunsets under a waterfall of passionate soul.
The sound of island music drifts in the coolness of
winter nights to warm the sands beneath.
A matrimony of wandering footsteps beneath lucid palms.
Bless the consciousness and enrich our gardens of poetic
landscape. To feel the lava warmth of home.
Fingertips yearning to explore the untouched. Savor the softness of
her lips… my thoughts adrift… my celestial mind of intimacy …
Shine your eyes of raven upon me.

Vintage Fabric

Imagine a moment frozen in time... two souls
blossoming into a romance of dreams...
Icy waterfalls cascading into steamy passionate streams...
Graceful movement upon frigid crystalline wading pools our hearts
pirouette... black swans of elegance in evening silhouette
White hula dress adorn her feminine curves... island pua in her hair
Lei of aloha gently lay upon her breasts
Snowflakes melt upon her warm silky flesh... sparkle in the moonlight
Visions of life's lost innocence
The fabric of earth, melody of poetic grace
Captured by far memory in vintage hourglass
When my lips touched to her face
Magnetic forces still guide us...
Our universe of stars still attract
Moments now frozen in time
Locked away in dormant heart
Pensive in silence her mind drifts... the solitude of the writer
Her pen lifts...to share the perceptions within
To thaw the cold of the comets between our two worlds. My mind
wanders with hers to taste the vintage... to find our rhythm of hearts
Walk among the Naupaka lined pathways that separate our souls.
Narrow the distance of our shores in luminescent shades of sand
Imagine a sunrise of poetic landscape that once again
illuminates the passion of the musician and poet.
Forever interwoven throughout the fabric of our earthen existence

Valentine Summer

Late summer eve over the windswept beaches of solitude I
await the greeting of warmth from a lady of purity...

Heat of passion soothes my mind from times long forgotten...

As familiar as the sound of ocean waves crashing upon my soul Embrace of
aloha penetrates me like a thousand arrows from the cherubs of heavenly stars

Painted sky of red splash across the horizon in hues of
brilliance to ignite lava flames in my heart.

Beautiful as the day of celebration a summer dream has gifted me the deepest
of Aloha. Endless stream of blissful harmony of souls. Fused together in the
nebulous of newborn stars our gravitational forces of attraction pull us closer
and closer. Resistance is futile in any attempt to break this spiritual bond.

Hands, body, mind and soul all become one in our commitment to the
stars that hold our names. Your heart forever etched upon my mortal
presence of this lifetime pulses inside me. It quickens and palpitates
the wild beating of my heart. I pursue the muse of my dreams this
eve as my Valentine summer slowly fades with roses of Autumn

Reminisce in the splendor of colored leaves of the forest. A truly
memorable summer of love my Valentine. You have gifted my
heart a place of sanctuary and gentle peace I surrender to you. My
arms tightly embraced in the passions of your lyrical verses

Never to be the same our lives spring eternal in
the odyssey of my Valentine Summer.

Me ke aloha
Pumehana

Tapestry

The tapestry of aloha to enrich my soul with the sweetest fragrance has graced my senses. It radiates with the warmth of the island sunrise. How this pua has captivated my every thought is hypnotic. The Hula of Aloha from the purity of your heart dances upon sands of time. It beckons me to your shores like a silken voice from the Makai.

A melody of passion soothes my mind and caresses my soul in a chorus of whistling palm fronds in gentle trades. Earth, moon and stars have stood still for our life paths to fill our canvas with the paintings of lyrical creativity from our soul. They have taken our hearts on the most enchantingly passionate journey my love. Are we for real or just a dream I remind myself? How does this lady of aloha captivate my heart? Her touch of divinity I discover more every day.

A scripture of aloha has long held me in your embrace as I have come to realize how my presence of heart has travelled with you your whole life. This is my missing part of life you have carried in earnest my island pua. Mahalo for caring and nurturing it for all these years for me to finally find your essence of spiritual guidance.

In tepid waters our eyes will meet under a crescent moon backlit by the stars you have so many nights wished upon. Waves crashing upon the shoreline we cradle the ache of our hearts until smiles of our eyes once again illuminate the beauty of aloha deep within.

Blessing of Friendship

Stars bend into prisms of rainbows
Strum my heartstrings for a girl I humbly adore
Shimmering down upon eyes of blue Makai
Heart filled with peace, joy and tranquility pours
forth a sweet fragrance of island lily
My musical heart feels her divine touch. A baptism of my soul

A blessing of friendship blossoms within
Her presence forever imprinted in spirit and hale
A hula girl graces her passion of friendship and aloha
Permanent impressions upon my flesh

An ocean mist fills my eye
My thoughts hold onto a lingering kiss.
The earthly paradise we share, lyrical meanings of expression
Form bonds of carbon to unite us on this journey
of reality and starship of fantasy

Palms slow waltz her Victorian heart among the moonlit Naupaka
Celebrate the cherished blessings of life's simple pleasures
Let's begin anew with the heart songs painted across our horizons
Color our passionate souls with indigo visions in our eyes

Our hearts converge in earthly dreams and starry realms...

Under the Banyan Tree

Tendrill strewn branches of the Banyan reach
Hawaiian heat of sun filters and dapples feet
Cooling fertile Naupaka vines and wild pua beneath
Shimmering sea of turquoise
Elegant with poise
Waves of Maui
Rolling west beyond Ka'anapali

Breach of whales crack whitecap
With gleeful eye
Tail slap
Pulse of distant darkness... mysterious Molokai
Puffy cumulous... languishing sky
Spirit of Pe'le in almond eye
Watching the world drift by

Dream with me beneath sacred Banyan
Roses congeal.. inebriant and surreal
Resurrect lost visions...
Beauty and mysticism
Hold me in your sturdy embrace
My earthly friend
My soulful companion

Toes burrow deep into white tepid sand
Cast a smile of enchanting glow
Shadow of my heart in gentle hand
Like breezy colors of rainbow
Beneath the shadow of the Banyan tree

Lovers love... poets dream
Pristine vision... most serene
Wanderlust and chest drumbeat
With my Polynesian queen
Passions of aloha
Under the Banyan tree

Raven Heart

Are you free tonight my ku'uipo to walk along the surf of Polihale?
Where emerald seas merge with the land of Barking Sands.
In silky white mist your heartbeats with the whisper of island charm.
Eyes dissolve into ravenous waves,
I gaze longingly into the evening tide.
A fragrance of memories come rushing back into my soul.
My shadow of Polynesian stars radiates in lanterns glow.
Splendor of serendipity is beyond the realm of earthly existence.
Summoned by dreams of coral sea. I am your creation from the
vastness of Makai of blue. Walk with your hand in mine. A matrimony
of wandering poets along windswept dunes of eternity.
Sing the harmony of soulmates etched into the NaPali cliffs for all
to witness the love story of celestial beauty. Undulating vibrations
of earths secrets we breathe Aloha. Footprints leave trace of a
journey blessed by devoted passion and dreams of romance.
Your heart... young and endearing my darling.
Impressionable but beats strongly.
Spirit of independence.
Lost to my touch its essence.
Withering thoughts like tulips in gardens of solitude rain.
Guarded and dormant.
Passionate in search of early warmth of Spring.
Thaw the frigid pulse of spurned romance and open life to new melody of song.
Seek new friendship and freedom of expression.
Follow the inclinations of artistic soul as they will
always be the test of honesty and guidance.
It is a shared wisdom of both to begin the renaissance of your raven heart.

Sea of Life

The sea of our soul's treasures lay deep within. Forever yearning in undying passion. Unspoken on the calm surface of human existence. Churning in ambitious creative energy below. Propeling desire, hope and aspiration of life and frail understanding of immortality.

When two souls collide in a language of expression of reality and dreams. A lazy river of currents flowing through lush palm valleys. A beautiful garden grows to weather the seasons and stormy disillusion of life. Together by natures grace they find strength, balance and intuitive friendship of aloha. A garden to nourish each other's breath and pathway through this life. Teach our derisive souls the virtues of God and spirit.

Walk in the ghostly footsteps of tidal sand of Ha'ula Bay. Stone statuettes symbolize the beauty of two souls born to share a bond of aloha. Eternal flames of unity our life minerals forged long ago in celestial stars now fallen to earthly realms.

The intimate relationship of moon, sun and stars is ours to cherish and behold its grandeur. Seek its guidance of infinite wisdom and revel in the lyrical melodies of orchestral beauty of the night. Illuminate the colors of poetic canvas and paint our imaginations across distant sunset and pastel horizons.

Where lost visions find the freedom of expression and artistry of passion.

Soul of Mirrors

The night breeze of faint memories drift across my eyes
Like moonbeams of faery tales against tassels of raven skies
Eyes lucid in turquoise rivers of light
Reflections in mirrors unite
A nebulous of photons of morning sunlight
Wetness of morning dew and honeysuckle bloom
Against my cheek her touch of fragrance and perfume
Inebriation of the sun and earth flower consume
Coursing veins and wild domains
Thrashing hearts locked in chains
Ignite embers of smoldering flames
A voice whispers my name
Sensual energy exude from droplets of soft rain
Embrace natures mystery of life and artistic design
Soulmates of destiny will always collide
In creations of light of new born stars fragile seedlings arise
Gardens grow in a reflecting glass of dreams and inhibitions
We look deeper into the mirror for our souls lost treasures
Destiny and fate combine
Search for clarity of vision like inspiration of art
Watch from distant moon our nights apart
Across depths of ocean and empty heart
Come to me my sunflower
Look into my eyes of indigo
Reflect your essence of smile and mystic power
Sing to me my muse of earthly divine
Enchanting melody beneath the sycamores
Symphony of aloha in our soul of mirrors

Blue Maha'ulepu

Are you free tonight my ku'uipo to walk among the stars of Maha'ulepu?

I emerge from my slumber from your beautiful eyes and heart
beating against me in romantic dreams of aloha

In the silky blue mist your body pulsates next to me in anxious breath and
womanly charms. Our eyes focus in a well of starry gaze into watery tide pools.

Fragrance of memories come rushing back into my soul. Polynesian star
radiates her glow along the mystic path to her heart. To feel her splendor
of aloha is beyond this realm of earthly life. Summoned by dreams of
your soul I am your creation from the vastness of Makai of blue.

I walk with your hand in mine... wandering poets along windswept
shores of Maha'ulepu. Sing the rhythm of soulmates etched into the
cliffs for all to witness the story of the kiss of the sea in undulating
memories of blue. Forever we create life in the footsteps of a journey.

I have kissed my island pua in her universe of stars. Searched the night sky
travelling past oceans of vast Makai. A story of fabled hearts. Cardinals sing
its melody in the trade winds. A glow upon her garden richness... sacred
sands and cliffs. Fertility of rainforest nurture sacred Naupaka vines.

Island soul and culture... allure her spell of Kauai. Hips of Hula saturate the
soul of rhythm. I have felt her passion, her touch, her fragrant hair of silk. The
sunlight of her morning smile and dreams of moonbeams. The grace of beauty
and solitude of devotion forever impressions in my soul of immortality.

Cradled and blessed am I in devoted passion and dreams of blue Maha'ulepu.

Gemini Falls

A poem of the stars immersed in consciousness comes
to fruition with the new moon tonight...
As my pastel pink and yellow horizon dissolves the sunset of the day
Vast ocean fades into darkness from richly blue and sight
A portrait of passionate souls envelops in silhouette
Intimate lovers left smoldering in afterglow of the Kauaian sunset
Together we ignite
Eternal flames amongst a billion stars light our journey
Magnetic fields attract and resonate with boundless polarity
Long silken hair draped across tan shoulders... firmness of breasts
Voice of texture, passion and intimacy
Depth of ancient tribal roots she exhales life's mystery
Soulful passions yearning for one another's touch and embrace
Distant hearts overflowing in a lunar tide of emotions
Tears flow through rivers of glittering stardust and wild honeysuckle streams
Beneath the palms her spirit of fragrance fills the
trade winds...a cool softness...aromatic
Breathing in her essence captivates
Her intuition speaks in whispering tones... She is special to this realm of paradise
Emanating purity of aloha and innocence
Flowing from rainforests of mystic trance... power of Hawaiian gods
Twin waterfalls of Gemini pour forth her multiverse of discovery and life
I sense her divinity
Dreamy touch upon my flesh her cosmic light transcends
Forever intertwined in tantric waves inscribe
Two hearts beat as one in harmony tonight
Lyrical waterfalls of Gemini our galactic energy combine

Lost in Paradise

Mountains in tidal moons of earth
Flicker of candle burns in lost desire
Worlds apart...Two hearts yearn
Valleys separate a love
always meant to be
Oceans divide the heavens
of ordained destiny
Mystics and muses of the
sea beckon sultry eye
Serenity of sirens of romance in song
Captivating in touch to entice
Never let go what is felt
true in beating hearts
Courtship of culture
Eternal vow of soulmates
A lovers touch never imparts
Never let go what is beholden
Life is too short to spend days not living
Secrets of truth
Peace and virtue
Brandish two hearts in
Forever youth
Melodies of aloha attract
Onyx of her eyes
Dark hair of raven

Irresistible touch and tact
Enchanted man
Good soul passionate mind
Hawaiian gods grant haven

Candlelight burns bright
When two friends illuminate
with essence of human life
Distance creates no barriers...
never a moment to hesitate
Shooting stars of passion
Limitless without boundaries
of time and space
Love transcends in
mythology of culture.
Ancient its emotion...yet grows
like wild Naupaka blossoms
Along the cliffs and ocean
Where happiness and aloha find
blessing in divinity of souls colliding
Ignite the eternity of paradise
Where two hearts belong
Gemini hearts beat as one
Like poets of romance
To forever write verse and song

Island Pua Left Behind

Intimate steps imprint themselves
upon one another in the crystal sands
of a time capsule sealed long ago.
Forgotten to all those who
walked tide washed beaches.
Except for two wandering
souls, lost poets of dreams.
In the warmth of Kauaian sunsets
hands intertwine. Snowy egrets
sing the melody of Kauai against
deep seas of blue makai.
A dream laden touch of wistful souls
temper our fever of love apart.
Together again tranquility of
gardens invoke fragrant passions.
Shade our eyes in prisms of rainbows.
Cool our flesh in shadows of romance.
We walk together in dreamy embrace.
Dance upon moonbeams
with the fireflies.
Eternal sands of Poipu, our souls
of creation and destiny.
The essence of pua in her hair lingers
in the soft island breeze. Memory of
aloha shadows me from across the sea.
Morning sun dances upon the
downward glances of her eyes.
Shyness of her smile, touch of silky
flesh... fabric of Polynesian soul.
She walks into my life with dreams of
passion... and poems only imagined.

My soul now trapped in
mirrors of reflection.
My island pua left behind
last summer...
Am I still living in her
dreams I wonder?
Does the heart still miss a beat
when our words meet?
Distance in us now starves
my cold blue heart.
Lost in translation how our
lives together fell apart.
As deep as her love... we
did not belong...
As deep as the Pacific
Our depth of song.
It was all wrong between
us but felt so right.
Emptiness of aloha fills my night.

My island dream left
behind last summer...
Do our eyes still meet her under secret
waterfalls and rainbows I wonder?
Walk with her under the
stars of Ha'ula bay?
Touch her soul in sweet surrender
upon the crest of ocean waves?
I hope there be a time I can find...
My island pua left behind.

I awake from a dream

Aloha Offering

She held back by inhibitions of the heart
Lost amongst a blizzard of cherry blossoms
Windswept rains of Spring start
Swirling dervishes
Angelic stars traverse in imagination
Drop back of smokie black
Beyond the pale of human comprehension
Lovers remorse saturate the mind
Dormancy of life I now find
Light years away withered inside
Like the offering of plumeria petals cast into ritual tide
Suspended... floating in nuance of watery facets
Dispersed in gratitude of tearful droplets
Emanate from misty eyes
Emotions pour from syrupy faucets
Rich ladles of maple sun and blue makai

The arc of lemon yellow chases the horizon
Seeds of creation begin new life
Blind direction in perfect vision
Cresting waves in whitewashed porcelain
Fatefully rooted upon fertility of the gods
Aloha spirit of connection
Flower peluls disseminate
Tidal moon forces beyond control
Divinity of command of nature and rule
Seek out new landscape of machinations
Carried by depths of oceans
Gravity of earth, sun and constellation
May mystic souls unite again to plant the seedlings
In her garden of Plumeria offering

Sunflower

Words cannot describe the mysteries of life
The attraction of her energy...
Like earths perpetual revolution around yellow sun
Golden sister moon in tow
The intimate dance of celestial origins
A lovers embrace of time, space and light coalescing
Wandering stars ignite as we met in dreams along
white sandy shores and surreal skies
Where poetic quills rest in reservoirs of ink wells of philosophy
The gravity of yearning hearts weigh heavy on my mind of feeble masculinity
To find inner peace and beauty is beholden to the journey of consciousness
To feel the warmth of another soul is the embrace of
the sun beams upon earthly sunflower
The light of existence and purpose each coexist in need of the other
Intertwined in cosmic destiny beyond the fathoms
of dimension and frail human destiny
Soulmates of the moons of astrological crossings
Beyond this planetary realm we share a common thread
Hearts interwoven upon the vintage fabric of Hawaiian quilt
Natures brilliance of fluffy cumulus above our head
Shade of the palms... dappled sunlight, sky of blue
Horizons disappear into seas of tidal moon
I shine upon the meadows in harmony with you
Caressing delicate petals of yellow and morning dew
We find solace in each other's touch my sunflower..
The mystery of me and you

Crescent Moon

I sense the billowing fascination of her passions
Like sails upon ships of our liaisons
Never could I ever fathom
Crescent moon, depths of starry oceans
Caress of waves and introspection
Drown my sorrows... a myriad of commotion
Inviting eyes overflowing
Smile radiant, soft lips beckon
Feminine flesh yearning
My enchantress my muse my goddess
Magnetic energy guide us
Explode into you my seed of desire
Celestial embrace like wild fire
Burn the dark woods of my kingdom
Permeate the landscape of this sire
New life spring forth in forest of green
Effortless attraction of gravity
Caverns of forbidden planets echo earthly dreams
Ripple like stones upon still water of mountain streams
Sprinkle like stardust through night palm leaves
Fullness of your breasts heave...deepening breath of pleasure
Pressed against me... softness of feather
Swelter with heat of summer weather
Bodies intertwined...
Captivates and blinds
Songs to be written...lyrics to find
Around distant rings of Saturn secret hearts combine
Congealed in cosmic rays... sparkle and shine
I adore your presence because you are mine
Like misty moon...
Crescent in your sublime 🎸

Whisper of Hanalei

Incandescent sands whisper with the moonrise over Hanalei tonight
Iridescent crescent moon bay shimmers in tranquil trades
Nene cackle in delight
Sunlight dissolves behind Bali Hai
Cathedrals of green disappear in labyrinth of grays
Jungle bird banter echo through lush mountainside
Surge of dreamy waterfalls dance upon eardrums
Natures pulse of Polynesia
Permeates my inner conscious with ambrosia
The essence of cultural beauty of the gods absorbed in layers of lava over time
Nestled in the rustle of palms and lazy river
Stars of Kauai shine
Holiness of devotion I pay her homage and bow of respect
Aloha blessings infuse me with sacred divine
Her touch of femininity flow like red wine
Through my veins
Inebriate my mind
A moment to touch the face of purity and passion in my fingertips
Feel the blossoming softness
The lavender of her lips
Gently grasping the movement of hula of her hips
Sleepy surfside turtles retire for evenings rest
We lay upon the sands of eternity by the grace of
creative virtue and dreams of immortality
Gaze upon the distant galaxies of infinite wisdom
And earthly truths
To enlighten the aloha within
By the whisper of the Hanalei wind

Tiger Lily

In the stillness of wintry blue the world floats by a window of dreams
Shadows of the moon tonight
Cast long shades upon the untouched snow
Lost Eden of northern candle flicker and glow

Impressions of aloha tapestries trapped in icy drifts
Frozen in time... moist full lips
Isolated from the heat of sun... caged heart and hips

Never to be held captive
Illuminant, ravenous tiger lily
Palpitates with smooth tranquility
Freedom of soul cannot be contained but forever reign

Polynesian song
Melt steely chains of mortality
Beneath the sway and bend of palm
Breathe in your essence my lily
Blossom in vibrant opal and orange

Fragrant smile of sensual beauty invites
Passion of souls ignite like
Secret touch of lei in gray lunar light

Simmering thoughts radiate from within
Eyes of opalescent shades of pleasure beckon
I touch and caress her smooth and subtle skin
Sinewy hardness pressed against hips blossoming
Captivates mind and body by light of the virgin sun
Curvaceous petals... feminine dexterity
Melt away inhibitions... flower of destiny

Mauka Cliffs

A wink of our eyes meet in blue brightness of mid-day surf
Sky born distant green of Mount Waialeale
Tropical winds of time whisper and churn
White drenched sands slip through the hour glass of hearts content
Solitude of souls collide and then dissipate
Passion free as birds of paradise
Gentle touch her lei of Aloha
Petals of silk drape beneath full breast
In softness and caress of island air
Hula hips of the Monarch dance
Interlope among vines of Naupaka and Gardenia
Flowing wings of her hula captivate in tropical song
Salty spray of sacred Maha'ulepu waves
Dissolving onto satin white rock shores... garden of seascapes
Vivid kaleidoscope and dreams
Enchants in tidal moons of spiritual odyssey
Rusty red royalty of Hawaiian gods
Intimate steps imprint themselves upon one another in the
crystal sands of a time capsule sealed long ago
Forgotten to all those who walked tide washed beaches
But for two wandering lost poets
Red Cardinals sing the melody of summer breezes
A dream laden touch of wistful souls temperate our fever of love apart
Shade our eyes in prisms of rainbows
Cool our flesh in shadowy cliffs
Waltz upon the clouds in dreamy embrace
Reflections of moonbeams in opulent space

Aurora Borealis

The coldness of winter wrath surrounds her warmth of soul tonight
Heart of passion radiates in waves of energy... Snowflakes melt
like buttery vanilla upon bronze shoulders and radiant flesh

Masculine heat of breath
Between firm silky breasts
My lady of northern star rise upon my horizon
Rest your eyes of raven passion in glittery facets upon my chest

Where snowy rivers melt into Kauaian waterfalls
Floating like plumeria petals in lush moonlit streams
Where natural curves meet my warmth of gentle fingertips
Sensual presence of extasy greets me in friendship of the night
Origins of souls find sanctuary and illumination
Aurora borealis of color and phosphorus glow
Force of nature, cosmic destiny, gift of sublime flow

Illuminate my soul with heat of a thousand suns
My northern star of colorful passionate light
Dance with me across distant oceans of might
Melt away inhibitions
Unleash the intimate fire of the gods that captivate
Fulfill our destiny of human desire and fate
Feel the emotion of strength of aloha
Snowdrifts melt as heat of northern star rise
In island dreams and heavenly skies

Water Dance

Polynesian waves wash upon moist lava rock in rhapsodic notes
Orchestral music of the earth
Ever conductive tidal droplets dance like tiny wayward sailboats
Baptism of passionate lilikoi sea gives life and rebirth

Pirouette in silhouette
Like the radiance of Hula girl in floral sundress
Bow in graceful pose of silvery wetness
I bear witness to the beauty of her Hawaiian sunset

Surging in pulse, undulating heartbeat
Mother nature exudes her precious gift unto humanity
Elements of life water dance
in serenity
Motions of oceans in harmonic beat and symphony

Bubbles of seafoam
Salty emerald spray
Misty blue makai and perfume of handwoven lei
Invoke idyllic mystery of intrigue in complexity
Formula of blending eccentricity

She entertains and comforts in vibrant soul
Watery my emotions to console
Beneath green palms of my slumber
Stars congeal in sweet surrender

Liquid facets dance like flowers in oceanic breeze
Backlit in fiery sunbeams
Fireflies of tropic sea
Her effervescent magnetic charm and energy

Candlelit Vision

Slumbering mind of passion so fragrant
Inhale the splendor
Inhibitions so vibrant
Her freedom reigns... born to be wild
Honesty of inquisitive child
Golden honeysuckle dreams drip like morning dewdrops upon ubiquitous hive
A Queens heart, soul illuminant
Eloquent, coquettish
Forever to traverse night skies her starship of the galaxy
Breathe in her life to create my earthly garden of mystery
A labyrinth of song and poetry
Governing my universe of perceptions and sanity
Reality or surreal conceptuality
A deepening impression of forgotten love
A charm of emotions and radiant energy
Her gracious invitation
A touch of virtue and immortality
Compels my being of human condition and illusory
Her body of stars lay against me in delicacy
Tone flesh of heartbeat pulses and vibrates eagerly
Candlelit warmth cresting effervescent glow upon eyes of blue sea
Mythical visions of Hecate
Woven into the fabrics of time convey her gypsy energy
Sparkle like stardust her songs of rhapsody
A symphony of orchestral beauty lay upon me
I am but a flickering candle along her path of wisdom and serenity
To awaken slumbering passions and minds of philosophy
Enlighten her with tender kiss of the sunrise and aloha spirituality

Dark Galaxy

Heavenly stars of dark galaxies collide
Ignite a divine inspiration of a young girls heart
Shimmering smile illuminates
Red embers of passion glow
Brightness of comets across blackened sky
Warmth of natural flicker of fireflies
Yellow hibiscus of iridescent beauty
Hers, a genuine soul sparkles with stardust upon humanity

Enchanting melody of mystery
Touch of sincerity
Compassion of Polynesia overflowing
Filling yearning hearts of destiny
Adrift in a river of constellations
Wash into the arms of a young girl's heart.

Me ke aloha Pumehana

Night Waves

Night waves climb the lava cliffs
Moonlight glistens on watery blue
Darkening shadow of palm
Audible texture of the Pacific echo a tranquil calm
Soothing waves ingratiate her essence
Carve her name in island song and riffs
Sea of melody
Ballet of orchestral stars
Dance upon tides of the milky way
Whispering fragrance of hibiscus hypnotize
Intimacy of the dark wind sighs
In balmy Hawaiian trades
Angelic voice in soft firelight
Ignite devilish passion in opal eye
Wetness of feminine desire
Touch my cheek... alluring lips... enchanting smile

Fathom of my soul pulses
Beneath branches of Banyan
Vastness of Waimea canyon
My beating chest convulses
Impressions of aloha
Engrave her initials

Walk the sandy shore of life's journey
Through darkening shadows of infinite energy
Captured in the hour glass of time and creativity
We share the beauty and mysticism of lost love
In cosmic rays of the galaxy
Night waves of aloha caress my memory

Sundress & Honeysuckle

Wild fields of sunflower beckon the nature of innocence
Raven eyes of wonderment
Inquisitive winged nature... fledgling heart bathing in morning mist
Across wavy meadow distant sounds of laughter adrift

Soulful glee... beauty of creation
Hours pass in suns trek past white puffy clouds shading patches of endless plains
Generous warmth of grandparent's love and admiration

Impressionable girl of gifted mind
Intelligence beyond worldly stars
Innocence of childhood dreams pour in abundance from her
sundress Stained of fresh picked flower and honeysuckle

Yellowed fingertips of a heart felt poet are born of the moment
Nurtured by life of the farm she transforms into a divinity of aloha
Poetry of the soul of imagination
A grace upon the earth cultivating humanity in golden sun
Dreams of innocence my soul aspires to touch once again

Gypsy Soul

Like the radiance of moonbeams in my eyes
Your majesty my Queen you continue to illuminate gray skies
With vision of truth in honesty we all must find
Simple human nature mired by fear and lies

We are the perception of our mirrors of reflection
A truth of divine spirit your presence beams of power and energies
Upon humble king and countrymen
Shine upon my castle of dreams and immortality

Her bloodline flows with truth in moonlit rivers of my heart
Prisoners we are of time and space
Constellations converge to find a lost symmetry of the stars
Captivating in essence

Waves of gypsy soul and ocean depths of Tarot cards
My muse of celestial beauty and moonlight
Illuminate the path through our garden of mystery

Reticent

The Makai of endless blue
Lapping bronze tone legs
Waves massage in nuance
Caress seashell anklets
Glisten in clear watery facets
Koa pick in silky locket's
Salty brine... oceans depths
Saturate lung, tissue, flesh, most divine
Lava rock reflecting mid-morning ray against NaPali cliffs
Pendulum of palm rustling
Red cardinals cavorting
Eyes of raven Polynesia
Desolate empty beach...searching
Quandary of emotion
Opaque visions
Sanguine sands of inhibition
Tethered rigid corals
Rushing tide of emotions
Erasing shadows
Impressions of dreams fade
Palpable taste
Marmalade
Lovers collide into stardust
Tall like island snowflakes
Tropical dreams
Melt upon tan shoulders and heat of flesh
Hunger and thirst
Incandescent... incessant
Reticent my tongue
Intensity... Kauaian sun alone with her
Benevolent one

83

Coconut Breeze

Tradewinds breathe the fragrance of the coconut palms
Lofting... deft hungry lung
Garden isle of liquid soul
Refreshes and calms
Lanterns of wayward stars shine down in verses sung
Inebriant fruit of aloha
Sun kissed energy and flavor
Nectar of romance
Palate my tongue to savor
Virgin taste of silky sweetness
Succulent breast... milk of innocence
Sun ripened...nestling in tussling fronds
She gives up her bounty of fertile fruit of delight
Gift of inspirational bond of earth and light
Coconut breeze waft across depths of serendipitous sea
Fill my heart and Ohana with ubiquitous ease
Filtering scent of alluring simplicity
Reminds me of loves lasting memory
Mouth wide open in awe and tranquility
Ingest grainy sustenance of life's vitality
Saturate winding rivers of internal discovery
Faraway dreams of coconut moonbeams
Tantalize my taste buds
Dissolving illuminate streams
Drink in her essence of mystic waterfalls and tropic suds
Music of the trees gently bend and sway
Grace my longing and thirst of heavenly white haze
Goblets of splendor and infinite waves
Coconut palm of the Milky-way

River of Palm

Fronds of jungle green
Reflections in still river serene
Heaven's gate of Kauai
Winding and sublime
Mauka green to the Makai

Filtering late day sun
Caress coconut laden shores
Bowing in attentive guard.. creations blessed soldiers
Labyrinth of placid waters
Peaceful harmony of aloha

Palm river take me home tonight
Before sunlight shades and memories fade
Balmy winds lift seabirds of flight
Under feathery warmth of gods wing and might

Pillars of divine spirit
Rooted in sacred soil and lilikoi
Walk along her garden pathway
Empress of emerald royalty

Botanical bounty of earthly realms
Inspiring spirit of human life
Purity of heart's guiding light
Impressionist hues
Pastel verse and psalm
Palm river take me home tonight

Misty Heart

Lay your soft essence of desire against me as you sleep tonight.
Starlit streams in dream laden clouds amongst the stars

Moonrise above calm sea sparkle blessings into sleep laden eyes.
Warmth of trades through palms filter with fragrance of orchid
Her touch of Lei never lost

Northern star rises in evening constellations
Shimmering lanterns from a poet's thought once read

Until the morning sun crests may your heart rest in slumbering tide
Awake to new found inner strength and intimate peace of mind

A new day to greet unknown horizons
May the Lei of Hawaiian blessing touch my island pua with Aloha

Moonlit Shadows

Her darkness of shadow remains
Eyes of raven cut from blades of onyx
A slice of Alice
Tuned and sonic
Hula girl awash in a wishing well of stars
A myriad of the Milky Way afar
Little dipper of sanguine ladles
Tarot cards and story fables
Like the moon of Io in Jupiter's gravity
Locked in steely tungsten
Dancing spirit
Elliptical forces of planet and sun
Touch like thunder snow in waves of porcelain
A polarity of freezing fountains
Flash frozen desolation of intuition
Look to the sun of the Polynesians
Melt the swords guarding ammunitions
Discard the weaponry that imprisons your freedom
Burgeoning black hole of hearts
Nothing escapes her visions
A meteor of change across the sky
Burns bright but quickly fades
Supernovas disappear in the blink of an eye
Atomic particle energy sprinkles like stardust
Confuse my senses
Celestial island love potions
Intoxicating my blood red moon on fire
Above vast horizon of south Pacific ocean
My quill dips once again
In our inkwell of slumbering passion

Tangerine

Crashing waves caress our tangerine dream
My enchanting muse of effervescent sea
Softness of stars your eastern glow
Almond eyes and genuine soul
Candle flicker and heart flow
Graceful presence of moonlight
Dance upon feminine shoulders
Shimmering stardust through silky hair my fingers
Fresh fragrance of gardenia perfume lingers
Filtering through my senses like a lost lover
Glistening lips my soul to discover
Tantalizing pleasure
Pulse of consciousness our heartbeat together
Time and space disappear
Passions collide in Earth's atmosphere
Angelic her touch of lilikoi tear
Rain down upon me in divine splendor
Chasing Chinese lanterns in the darkness of sky
Drift away with me
My tangerine dream tonight

Beautiful Kauai

I miss her garden realm of existence
Windswept notes blending in tones
Blossom in earthly attraction
Across towering mountain and sapphire ocean
Shaded eyes capture a mystic vision

Cast in leeward cliffs... scribed into etchings of lava stone
she ponders earths scripture... poetic quill resonates
Emotions felt deep in dreams of soulmates

Faraway star of Ha'ula bay awaits
Gentle smile of rainbow and pristine ferrous gates
Echo through cliffside canyons riotous waves roar
Leaves a whispering sound upon unwavering heart torn

The taste of coconut salty mist beading soft bronze skin
Delicate it's sensuous flavor of aloha...
Pure Kauaian
Humpbacks delight with splash of tail fin
Spinner dolphins greet the sunrise in spirit of hula dance
Frolic in waves of hypnotic trance

The infinite courtship of earth, sun, life of the sea
Soothes my dreams in timeless artistry
Fascinates my soulful journey of discovery
Palates of creations pastoral imagery
Beautiful Kauai

Me ke aloha

Another Day's Fire

Relax your mind, body and spirit in my soothing rush of warm ocean
currents. Beyond Jupiter's distance of fabled stories of lush romance.
Into a cosmos of anthracite and exponential universe.
Shifting sands of yearning thirst of consciousness.
Contemplating the natural love that seeks to root between us.

As dreams unite in a verse of friendly rhyme and intimate discourse.
We share a vision of the tides of resolve in softlit waves of companionship.
Driven by fate and human diligence of existence.
Evolutions of sun will shine its light to guide us.
Ripen our fruit of vine in Spring flowers of earthly wine.

My inspiration, a poetry of my heart in a spirit of her rising sun.
Goodnight my love, may your eyes of opal rest in
the silk quilt of Chinese fabric spun.
Wrap you in dreams of feminine charm and eloquence.
Beneath the moons of Neptune and stars of Aquarius.

Till we embrace in the embers of another day's fire of romance.

Blue Ballet

Salty spray of the ocean thunder crash upon the North shore in a winter
swell Pacific surf surging upon sandy shores and island longboards
Waxed and tuned skating big waves in a orchestral ballet of blue
No fear to be felt in the lion's roar as gelatinous waves consume
Floating with a chaotic fragrance of Hawaiian perfume

Slicing curves in the arc of liquid turquoise tenacity
Inner strength of passion to dominate and conquer
Riding nature's wake of Polynesian artistry
In stormy seas of late December
A solstice of the sun, earth and soulful energy
Command her touch of smooth caress
Wayward dolphins water dance in pods of complexity
Diving in distant whitecaps of foamy density

Toes grasp tightly upon the Koa wood beneath
Velocity of acceleration pushing fast across tropical coral reef
Inertia of lunar currents rise like titans trampling lava shores
Gravity of the heavens in full control unleash her wild boars
Test the virtue of all who tempt her fury
In a wake of tumultuous tides of demonic demagoguery

Rigors of the soul harden with desire and integrity
Fate guides the heart and direction of human immortality
Drifting in a reverence of self being castaway in
a labyrinth of oceanic mythology
In footsteps of the ancients of Huna philosophy
In search of the perfect wave of spiritual identity
In a ballet of blue and emerald sea
To inebriate the pulse of pumping arteries

Chasing Rainbows

A refraction of light from above shines down upon
Mauka of green flora and waves of blue beyond
A smile of nature's energy arching across sleepy horizon
Raindrops dancing against supple fabric of wet tone bronze
Chasing rainbows in a cool shower of an island song

Myriads of color and soulful tone
Alluring like the silhouette curves of her back against white sandstone
Arch of feminine mystique in faceted haze
Iridescent spectrum of Aloha conveys
Melts into my clouds of stormy grey
To lift my beat of heart on a new day

A mother's touch to calm the spirit of humanity
A cohesiveness of inner consciousness and natural beauty
Filters like dappled sunlight through breezy palm tree
Painting the imagination of hope and individuality
Permeating passion of sumptuous slumbering dreams
A divinity of spirit of Huna philosophy

Primary colors of the universe Backlit with essence of vanilla sky
Evocative presence of wavelengths in her eyes
Enchanting treasures await to enrich my bride
Captivating like the warmth of summer fireflies
A hue of coral reefs glistening in saltiness
Inviting with a warmth of black pearl eyes tracing down smooth thighs
Slender skin radiates with the gentle fragrance of life
Chasing rainbows across her deep oceans of soft crescent tides

Cherry Blossom 🍒

The gardens of Spring lie dormant Stillness of her heart lay in restful silence
Sun of Mandarin rises to caress earthen valleys of late winter essence
A warmth of rebirth from a new touch of Aloha
A spirit to convey the truth of emotion
Blessed by the graceful hand of God of unspoken reverence

She emits a divine artistry of light
As cherry blossoms awaken from cold deep slumber
Filling my branches of stark lumbering curves of timber
Vibrant pinks and snowy white
A carnival of color in parades of annual celebration

Her fragrance envelops the early morning breeze in
petals of Asian perfume and Zen infusion
Sturdy limbs and anchored roots come alive in pastel vision

She decorates my life design and inspiration
Flowers of natural selection and fascination
Ignite our pulsing beat of longing obsession
Taste of summer fruit awaits the soul of patience
As the heat of rising sun illuminates
Nectar of the stars of exuberance
My firmness of roots hold her tightly
with absorbing friendship

Endless lazy rivers feed my ocean of memory

Navigating the sea like wayward Clipper ships on the high tide
Sailing across a universe of destiny
The affinity of hearts will always collide
As the fertility of life blossoms in silky grandeur
Dancing rhythm of lyrics and surreal kiss of celestial allure
In gentle waves of opal and blue wonder
Beneath the cherry trees of her sacred orchard will forever endure

🎸

Collision

Musical notes fluid of soul reverberate in her presence of celestial magnetism
Vacillating in a immortal force of liquidity of eternal
seas washing through my veins of inflection
Invoking life's sacred pageantry upon the thirst of eyes of blue imagination.
Raindrops of cool late Summer showers fall upon
us through psalms of poetic fashion

Reflections of emerald green... simmering infatuation
Shimmering fire and ice... shooting stars of dimension
Convey a luminous awakening... warmth of lush vision
Lyrics of the Makai dancing with a melody of sweet Kauai rhythm
Sifting through my consciousness her gypsy eye of heart filled mysticism
A sensory deluge of hungry yearning perdition
Fanatical dreams of feathery softness in my hands of obsession
Trembling fingertips and muscle of sinewy hardness of attraction
Eternal flames crackle and burn in hearts afire of lustful libation
Spellbound my soul of earthly gravitation

A plenitude of firm ethos of undeniable devotion
Planting the seeds of embryonic synergy of romanticism
Floating on the fables of Polynesian passion... seas of subtle touch of creationism
Divinity of our faiths immortal reign of spiritualism
Vastness of the universe drifting in lucid sublimation
Immersing our toes in sandcastles of imagination
Unbridled heavenly stars possessing me in her meteoric stone of collision

Diver

Her mystery pulsates through arteries and every vein
My wayward traveler of romance and earthly domain
Chasing vivid dreams in a passion of immortal reign
Find your journey of solace in my embrace from distant heartfelt pain
Dance with my essence in gardens of Spring rain
Illuminate my shadows of the moon in crescent wane
Dive with me into seas of creamy smooth waves
Frothy and wild in frenzy passions of ethereal haze
Unleash our adventurous souls in effervescent ubiquitous daze
Enrage our emotions of sensuality impossible to contain
A grasp of feminine power in beating heart brave
In the virility of tropical winds of your soulful hurricane
Forever to revolve in memories of love sustained

Dive into my waves of soulful adventure anytime my love
Let me wrap you in my tides of dreams of mountain Laurel
Envelope you in a caress of vibrant colors of clear ocean coral
Dance with your intoxicant flavor of emotions
Show me your expert skill and talents to navigate my terrain of wild oceans
Rock my undersea kingdom of passionate adventure
We gaze upon sugary eyes with inductive stare
Stroking the jet black hair behind her left ear... my touch sincere
A romance of the sun kissing the waves on new horizons
as we surf in majestic journey of no fear

Me ke Aloha Pumehana😙🌺

Euphoria ♡

Her soft lips drift across opulent Polynesian sky
Implanting the seeds of her soul of Makai
Where sacred heartbeats of pulsing red conspire
In a gentle morning rain beading upon her flesh of rosebud
Blossoming in a dynamic myriad
A fragrant breeze of luxurious island spice
Across her oasis of palm shaded waterfalls
Alive with melody of mourning dove

The world stands still as we dissolve into cool ocean mist
A moment frozen in the stars of a longing kiss
Our intimate souls immerse
Impressionist hues of her loving touch
Brush strokes of Renoir down my neck and chest
Her artistry of emotion saturates my existence
A plethora of charm and enchantment
Taste of sweet congruence

Euphoric eyes radiate in a dreamy haze
Invite my caress of subtle blues against her steamy green and lucent gray
Spirits intertwine with torrential rushing waves
Exotic nature and nectar that I crave
Surging wetness of rainbow tides of virility
Lost upon her essence of romance and intimacy
Passionate souls unite in feverish crescendo of raging pageantry

Inhibitions fade as my forest fires rage
Release our destiny locked in celestial cages
To dance with her aura of feminine sage
Across rich valleys my temptation invades
Delicious honey drips like dew from Tulips of splendor
Pollinate her garden oasis in tranquility of sweet surrender
Where seedlings of earth and sky float in fertility of divine rivers

Fathoms of the Heart ♡

Island dreams beat in rhythm of the sapphire breeze
Lazy coconut palms drift in the caress of the soft windward trades

Monarchs of flighty melody dance upon temple
psalms as the heavens menagerie fades
Like the hazy tails of comets
Across a hemisphere of nature's promise I confess
Her musical serenade washes through my ocean valleys of distance

Her touch of orient enchants with a charm of subtle perfumed elegance
Unveils her inviting eyes in a emotion of alluring consciousness
In the wells of attraction and seas of wilderness
Two souls swirl in fathoms of romance
Lost in the aroma of yellow and red Hibiscus
Spiritual in energy of the dreamcatcher's starry web of the universe

A song to embue the lyric of my wandering imagination
To dip my pen in the morning honey suckle of wet dewdrops of passion

Dissolving words into the tropical mist of a secluded waterfall

Drenching our souls of fascination as treasures of rainbows call
Spirit 's coelesce in the gravity of Jupiter and tridents of Neptune
Basking in the reflective light of the galaxy of glimmering agents of fortune

Woven in the fabric of life and breath of lung
Verses of elucidation and magnetic principles blend in harmony forever sung
Our bodies sealed in a eternal grace, mercy and wisdom
To carve our caverns of an ancient premonition
We share this culture of special intuition
Ignites the torches of our journey through time and earthly season
To unite our lush garden landscape of Aloha in fathmic fascination

Fire of Love

Such a pleasant thought and wish to share on this rainy late winter night.
A scent of tropic perfume floats in my memory of lyric I'm compelled to write.
Wishing wells of stars streaming across our universe of emotion.
Fills the heart with yearning passion.
Souls of divinity and magnetism.

Seas that blend in warm tides of blue.
As the turtle drift and sleep in her soft sands of lush Ma'haulepu.
Dolphins dancing in slow rhythm of a reggae groove.
The fire of love burns in her heart with the Albatross of the full moon.

We ignite the earth beneath in thermal waves where Pele's desire consumes.
Simmering in soft trades through coconut palms in slack key tune.
Lips whispering my name in the notes of lyrical island psalm.
Glimmering in suspension of the stars above lost in her enchanting song.
A King and Queen aloft in a kingdom of nobility whose souls belong.

We search the horizons of our souls sacred waters.
A ritual of the hearts beat and fever.
The fire of love unites the rivers of destiny and rhythm of natural order.
Like the familiar touch of memory and intuitive understanding.
We share the blessing of life's celestial artistry and intimate wanderings.
Where the spirit of Aloha envelopes our garden of fruit ever expanding.

Gravity

I awake from a dream vision of her morning eyes of passion.
Showering radiantly as the comets of Geminids in the celestial
embrace of our intrinsic love fade from vision.
A collision of destiny of fervor and romance of the
planets and moons swirling gravity of emotion.

A solar wind powered of the suns rays glisten and breeze
through my heart of tangled introspection.
Billowing our impassioned sails of ships on the infinite waves of blue ocean.
A voyage of the soul we embark upon the thirst of illuminant spiritualism.
Hands clenched in the edifices of stoney ruins of ancestral perception.
Forever carved into the rigid cliffs of our holy communion.

The galaxy of the unknown wandering above in
secrets of starry softness of conception.
Where destiny's child of life awaits in endearing consecration.
A dream pervades in the heart of gentle meadows of butterflies of illusion.
To immerse the mind in theories of supposition.
We emboss the scriptures of eternal disposition.

Across the vastness of deep space and quantum equations of mathematicians.
Philosopher's query in the tranquility of origins of indelible soul of inquisition.
Sorcerer's cast their spells of magical mysticism.

King's and Queen's march in the palisades of royalty of indoctrination.
Knights of the courts of Windsor carry the loyalty
upon the shields of bronze idealism.
Together we build our majesty of the universe inextricably
sewn in the fabric of life and creationism.

Harmonic

The whispering sky of constellation calls me... notes
resonating with the music of my island Wahini
Ohi'a lehua petals float in a sea of infinite mystery
Galaxies of the night rain down in starry fountains of majesty
Graceful breeze upon her fertile green valleys of serenity
Depth of songful melody echoes across shadows of intimacy
Forever hearts torn between our twin horizon and dreams of soulful immortality

Harmonic convergence of charm and compassion
Hot lava pours from my heart of distant consolation
Magnetic resonance of masculine terrain in seismic eruption
Rivers of Kilahuea flow wildly into her calm ocean tides of white ash pageantry

Orange yellow glow dissipates into waves of blue posterity
A release of steamy emotions evaporate in billowing
clouds of passion and promiscuity
Igneous rock of Polynesian gods bless new land Give rebirth to wild flower fields
Blending in familiar wind the aromatic perfume of
Malayan coconut... our palm seedlings yield

Souls cling to ferrous mountain gates and towering spires of sacred NaPali
To grace the cheek of the heavenly divine and inner consciousness
Together we share a moment of life's tapestry
The culmination of nature's fury and artistry
A plethora of intimate allure
Whispering souls cast in moonlight of the Winter solstice
Her touch reigns upon me in tranquility beneath shimmering stars of astrology
We plant our garden of earthly seeds of harmonic destiny

Her Majesty 🌷

Her jewels sparkle with the radiance of moonbeams
in subtle rays of turquoise of my eyes.
Your Majesty my Queen you continue to illuminate in opalescent painted skies.
A mythical song of Aphrodite in a ministry of gospel of the sea.
Simple human nature attracts in the lunar gravity of tides of intimacy.

We are the perception of our mirrors of reflection.
The truth of divine spirit in the presence of nature's power and institution.
Upon humble knight and countrymen.
Shine upon my castle of dreams and Lavender laden garden.
Where your decadent fragrance flows in lazy rivers of my throbbing pulse afar.
Prisoners we are of time and space apart.

Astrologies collide to behold our symmetry of the stars.
In the aura of gypsy soul and ocean depths of Tarot cards.
Fate unveils its mystery of the beat of a impassioned heart.
My muse of celestial beauty and moonlight.
Dance with me upon your Hawaiian quilt tonight.
A royalty of island memory in the Kalaheo night.

Her Smile

Across hemispheres of hazy cumulus
Her smile radiant, eyes of opal shimmer with stardust
Bold orchestral orb connects us
Taste of amber honey and velvet yellow hibiscus
Float in heavenly streams of sunbeams of the universe

Familiar like song notes caress
Absorbing ray of illuminance
Swimming in a tapestry of
magic runes our cosmic being
Earth and sun coalescing

Blessing hearts and minds as we intertwine in the fabric of time
A destiny of circumstance
Fate and prophecy bring our souls together in renewed friendship
Intuitive emotions of a past life of lost romance sift through my consciousness

Filtering through the hourglass sands reveal her Asian mystery
To reunite the warmth of souls of passion and intimacy
Instill the inspiration and poetic touch of a divine artistry
Compelling my heart in waves her attraction of sunlight on distant seas

Like a lyrical nectar upon my lips her sweet flavor of honey
A breath of fragrant Plumeria through the sway of lazy palm trees
Like the gentle touch of a summer breeze
Her smile graces my presence with painted charm of spiritual serendipity

Imaginary Kiss 🫦 ♡ ♡

The innocence of Aloha in her caress saturates my heat of flesh
In the morning sunlight her smile crests with the warmth of South Pacific
Wet with the morning dew of mystic spirit
Upon her precious pouty lips
Greets me with the gentle sound of languishing waves in her ocean song as we kiss

In dreams her softness
So close but I cannot touch
I can see, I can hear but I cannot feel your breath
It's there, it's real
I wanted you all my life
My heart beats in chaotic motion
In surreal sensuality from her imaginary kiss

Let me cuddle next to your soulful attraction
My lady of passionate adoration
Your eyes of pearlescent sparkle and calm my heart of infatuation
Shower me with the intimacy of feminine mystery Mon chérie
Your life energy calling me
Fill me with your inspiration
As our stars collide in a bastion of celestial beauty

A premonition of love radiant and true
Lost romance and passion consume
Permeates with mythic power of thunderous boom
Across the hemispheres of my mind
A blessing to my soul of artistic design

Alluring lyrics... enchantingly haunting
Wandering thoughts.. exotic and exquisite
Dreamy sunsets of intimate charm
Lips of sugar cane fields... I long for you
Moist with supple fullness in her sultry dress
Bodies pressed and intertwine... embracing in the frothy ocean mist
Imaginary kiss... of my lady of stone amethyst

🎸

123

Intimate Truth

The night hemisphere of timeless
mystery drifts with the gentle sea.
Spectacles of the galaxy glimmer
in effortless dynasty.
A spirit of savory spice drips like soft
rain upon the thirst of island memory.
Like a chord strummed by her touch
of Orchid fragrance of melody.
Manic my depth of emotion and
homage of Polynesian passion of poetry.
Intrinsic souls of Aloha radiate
its charm and eloquence with
the new moon of February.

Calm trades banter with the call of
Sandpipers dancing with the waves.
Twinkling stars intertwine in the
fading orange and yellow marmalade.
Soffiting upon the heart in
slumbering serenade.
Blending our seven seas, drifting
Sonnets of blue and onyx escapade.
Dreams dance upon the shores
as long shadows fade.

The sun kissed ocean of Ni'iha
sparkles on diamond crystalline
depths of emerald and blue.
Filling our senses of life's true
anatomy of soulful gratitude
A precious journey of awakening
unveils beneath the heavens
of our intimate truth.
Hearts converge in the crucible of
Pele's fire and currents of Kanaloa
to bare our ripening fruit.

A magnificent element of design
and congruence of soaring
emotion and rising altitude.
Basking in the elation of my
consciousness of precious creation.

We gaze upon the constellations in its
immortal force and infinite maze.
To write our songs of romance beyond
earthly realms of wintry days.
The sorcerer's apprentice casts
it's spell upon the palms of
shadowed hearts of pain.
Creating our path among the gardens
of secret passion our lives engage.
Palpitating my soul in a
insatiable rage. Hungering for
her precious ellixor of love and
friendly thoughts pervade.
Against my chest her touch of Lilikoi
tears of revelation... like supple
rain upon the wings of the Dove.

A freedom of expression
extrapolates in my eyes of
blossoming cherry orchards and
perfumed skies of white cotton.
Bonds of magnetic energy
soothing and rhythmic.
The music of her sacred symphony
of caress wild and seismic.

Liquid Soul ♡ 🌊

My heart wanders in her footsteps of island sand beneath the sway of night palm.
Listening to the music of heart songs calling across her ocean of calm.
Like a lyrical melody of liquid soul summoned to destiny.
Guided by constellations of starlit eternity.
In seas of pure emotion
of a Polynesian love story.

Embroidered across heavenly body her wings of feathered angelic motion.
Delight my feverish fingertips in savory allure
A taste of purity on pouty lips dujour.
Soothe my desire as we lay upon her labyrinth shore.
Arms locked in celestial embrace of time and space.

A radiant charm of nature's serenade washes away the distance of hemisphere.
Her silhouette in moonbeams.
Glistening with toned muscle of slender bronze flesh and long shimmering hair.
Filling my heart with a effervescent smile of gleam in the thickness night air.

Lost in a fragrance of inebriant royalty.
Drifting in the pungent salty breeze.
A soothing harmonic complexity.
Strumming my chords with her intimate symphony.
Her waves dance over me in lunar tides of liquidity.
To immerse the heart with waves of blue fantasy.
Where the earth and super moon kiss upon the sea.
Shaping the oracle of divine artistry in sculptures of lyrical poetry.
To ignite our dreams of passion in meteor showers of the galaxy.

Lofty Verse

Follow your hearts inspiration and journey of spiritual awakening
Inviting as the cathedrals of reign precipitating
Dancing on cumulus of fragrant Polynesian songs of romance
Surrendering to our bonds of destiny and circumstance
Swept away in a landslide distance
Her irresistible endearing glance

Long shadows cast upon the earth reach deeper than southern ocean
Like ripple of stone upon still water of dreams in slow motion
Reverberate in holy matrimony of verse and intimate frequency
Orchestral stories of serene audibility

A masterpiece of nature's serenade intertwines
To tie our distance in heavenly sustenance
A lioness roar echoes in passionate pride
Calling me to her canyons of charming lair
In seductive notes and long silk of Asian hair
Knots my body and fingertips of twisted heart
A rip current of turbulent sea tearing me apart
She purrs in my touch of hard muscle and poetic art

Overflowing her lustful intrepid floodgates
Spilling down her crescent smile in savory white consummate
Across surreal hemispheres of our intimate pace
A frenzy of fire in my strength of arms her soft fabric of lace
Bound by a sensuality around her wrists
She surrenders to my intimacy of lofty verse

Love and Lucidity 🖋♡

May windswept dreams of whispering lips gently caress you in soft moonbeams.
Dance with the spirit of the Albatross in destined flight.
Dissolve our souls into a sunset horizon slowly fading into cool of night.
Reverberate in poetic waves of mystery.
Yearning in soft cadence upon the cliffs my siren of the sea.

Together our sails billow freely as we sail upon the thirsty waves.
In fruitful desire and fate of passion that never fades.
Long strokes of our oars rotate and move in perfect symmetry.
Upon the smoothness of a mountain lake of serenity.
Melting into the wilderness of love and lucidity.
Enchanting treasures lay deep in her depths of discovery.

May our worlds gravitate in orbits of acendency.
Resting beneath the starry fires of eternity.
Beyond the touch of mortal aspiration of humanity.
Looking deep into our eyes of onyx and tides of blue.
Dark waves of anthracite of chisled hearts beat in tune.
Autumn leaves transcend nature's bounty in painted array.
Souls unite on the leeward energy of Pacific trades .
Together we rise on new winds of change.
Stoking the embers of our intimate flames.
Soothing the warmth of bonfires in our eyes.
Burning with intensity beyond our earthly realms.
Breathing in the flowers of the dawn of a shared sunrise.

Mandarin Sunrise

Crest of morning light above mountain and sea
Radiant across the hemisphere of simmering mystery
Coalescing aura in a heaven of stars
Slow dissolving shadows fade away with the moons of Mars
Mandarin sunrise reflects upon realms of innocence and fate
Opal eyes and shimmer of Auburn hair gravitate
Her fire burns deep upon my earthly embers
Flames of orb ignite the passion of soft breath of lips
Inviting as the touch of slender lover's fingertips

The wandering poets pens share a inherent bond of friendship
Convey a deeper meaning and blessing of life and Aloha
A dream upon the drift of constellations lightyears gone
Romancing my heart of diamond cut from black Carbon
Like the flowers invite the rise of early morning sun
A voice of charm, A harmony and blessing of song

We cannot control our fate of passion or spirit of intimate discovery
But to embrace its blessing with those we find peace, happiness and generosity
I can only convey my honesty of soul as emotions of creativity
A natural bond of elements congeal in prisms of color and light
Illuminate new pathways and unlock the doorway and meaning of life
We inhale the oxygen of existence
To express our lyrical nectar upon each other in
waves of orange and yellow Hibiscus
Blossoming in orchards of rain beneath Asian cherry trees that bare witness
Our affection of enchanting energy between us

Moonshine

My eyes drift in a cascading mountain stream of her touch of suppleness
Spirits caress and wander valleys beneath enchanted sunsets
Like dream laden dolphins dance with the wings of the Albatross
Drink in the glow of nature's divine luminance
Coalesce in a history of creation and inspirational vision of renaissance

A love to strum my sleepy heart of poetic verse in pure magnificence
A chord of sacred passion to lift my sails into silky clouds of nebulous
Stirs my direction of stars of an adolescent kiss

My mind stirs like copper kettles of moonshine on the southern Carolina mist
Winds aloft of the whiskey corn mash through deep hollows of forest
Inebriates my senses with her waves of sweet romance

Her fragrance triggers the heart... filtering through
the Hickory trees of remembrance
On the backroads of my mind a familiar smell of lush Mountain Laurel fragrance
My heart of Dixie innocence
Swimming in the aroma of her river morning mist
Blending songs of melody weave our story of fate and fertile elements
Migrating on the boundaries of soulful consciousness and natural laws of science

Muse ♡ and Musician ♫

The radiance of her eyes of onyx melts into my riversong of whispering emotion.
Floating like blossoms on the currents of romance
in novels of windswept imagination.

A softness of skin of oriental silk draped across my chest and soulful disposition.
A rawness of attraction and alluring intuition.
Moonbeams blend in our intimate temples of thought and fascination.

Natural melody of Asian passion glows in long dark strands of mane.
Calling me into the night hemisphere of her subtle fragrance of domain.
Chivalrous knight stands guard her treasures and kingdom of nobility.
A temptress in a churning sea of surging waves
her seductive ambiance of femininity.
My songstress of evocative inspiration.
She is the elation and magical spell of island poetry.

We paint the Matisse of our lives upon the iconic notes of a Mozart's symphony.
Luminant in the sensory perception of our mirrors of lucidity.
A versal liturgy of sweet eroticism.
Brushes of the artist in cirrus clouds of pastel impressionism.
Our worlds come alive in lyrics of new found passion.
A muse and her musician.
A magnetic energy soothes our harmonic touch of
enchanting discovery of lush vision.

Glistening lips caress as fingertips impress across
her fertile seas of blissful sublimation.
Her sensuous touch of gentle trades upon my sails of masculine attraction.
We share the chance of fate and power of nature's pureness of spontaneity.
Souls of eternal love savoring the wine of vineyards of Lombardy.
Resolves in the warmth of the vintage oak and burgundy.
Dissolves upon our palates of intimate solidarity.
Stars of destiny unite in the rising sun of far eastern dynasty.

Nebulous

A Tahitian wind of memory floats in my southerly Pacific trades
Across the vastness of ocean waves
Her subtle smile crests with the arc of dolphins in a palisade parade
Calling my spirit to a faraway arch of palm and coconut honey marmalade
Deft congruence of the seas and moonlight serenade

Natural attraction of chemistry
A relativity of the soul
The artistry of human expression
Constantly revolving around a nucleus of internal dimension
The nebulous of our galaxies of formation
Forged in lava fields of cohesive design shape our
burning pursuit of happiness and passion
Chasing the island dreams of the heart of malleable impression
Flames spark the fire of wandering ambition

A synchronicity of life and heavenly transition
adorn her handwoven coral shell necklace
A interlude of thought and spiritual wonder
A clarity of sky above as we meet upon the sands and blue thunder
A Tahitian drum beats in rhythmic meter
In a thirst beneath the nights liquid amber
Hearts awash in the tidal bioluminescence
Pulsing like the electrons of fateful elements
Ionic bonds of our planetary existence

Random selection of the universe
Unites the particles of gravitational force of energy and sunlight
Combining strength in a tandem intricacy of divine rivers and currents of might
A nebulous of spiritual Aloha and invocation of mother nature's purpose
Her fury and charm relentless
A nuance of intimacy and soulful acquiescence
Tracing her Hula hips of graceful movement lost in the salty mist
Our worlds collide into the birth of new stars and heavens of futurist elegance

Night Rain

A placid rain of a island spirit falls through my fingertips and willow of palm
Blessing soil and sacred stone beneath with an aura of richness
Into my vastness of ocean calm
Dissolving a lost innocence of memory
Like notes of a faraway songbird across a forest of dreams
Calling through the shadows of gray skies
Misty wet melody melt upon my rocky streams

Crashing upon seas and rigid cliffs of majestic pride
A locomotive energy of a incessant lunar tide
Stand firm and resistant to the erosion of emotion and conflict of desire
A collision of elements of the earth, wind and stars of natural divinity
Forever locked in battlefields of gravity and diversity of human ideology

Droplets bead and caress the soul of immortality
With teardrops of Aloha and compassion
Moisten her leaves of lavender and island spice
Touch upon my cheeks with teasing intimacy
Wandering clouds of fate and prophecy
Waltz beneath the atmosphere of our embrace
A river of the realms of time and space
Flowing in unison with the arc of double rainbow

Truth of heart prevails in forges of burning passion
Tempered by the softness of gentle cool showers of heavenly creation
A longing of the soul to touch the face of God
Droplets of mother nature's vision
Trace down her face of inspiration
Inhaling the beauty and essence of gypsy mysticism
Pulsing heartbeat in the falling night rain

Nobility

She is as gentle as the island Hibiscus...a palate of the
evening sunset dissolving into the dusk
Our celestial embrace reigns upon us in facets of glittery stardust
A voice of Mandarin silk lays upon my trembling
flesh... drowning in the sea of intimacy of lust

My veins pulse in a tribal connection with her ancestral comets
Like the universe opening its garden of insatiable fruit to my lips
A sensuality laced into my destiny
Woven through time in a Laureate wreath of King's nobility
She intertwines with a passionate love of nature's fertility

I consume her fruit in mass of gravity
Savoring its juice... ripe upon my lips in my chalice of victory

Come to my Kingdom and explore my adventures
of a Queen's alluring spirit of gypsy
Cauldrons of stars set our intimate blood aflame
Dancing with fire of the galaxy of our Milky Way

Surfing my waves of tidal liquidity with deft skills of smoothness
Druid soul of compassion
I want to get lost in her languishing touch of ocean song
Chasing shooting comets to write my tales of fabled emotion
Whispering skies pour with silver ladles of moonbeams
Upon desert wind the thirst of two hearts of devotion
Brighter than a billion stars she lights my universe of creation

Oasis

Soft lips drift in wind songs of Polynesian sky
Implanting the seeds of fruitful desire
Into sacred heartbeats of pulsing red blood
Where gentle morning rain beads upon flowering rosebud
Fragrant breeze of aromatic spice
Blossoming in a dynamic myriad
Across her oasis of palm shaded waterfalls
Alive with melody of mourning dove

The world stands still as we dissolve into cool mist
A moment frozen in the stars of a longing kiss
Intimate souls immerse
Impressionist hues of her touch
Brush strokes of Renoir down my neck and chest
Her artistry of emotion saturates my existence
A plethora of charm and enchantment
Taste of sweet congruence

Her eyes radiate in a dreamy haze
Invite my caress of subtle blues against her steamy grey
Legs intertwine with torrential rushing waves
Exotic nature and nectar that I crave
Si'l vous plait
Surging in waves of rainbow arcs of virility
Lost upon her essence of romance and intimacy
Passionate souls unite in feverish tides of pageantry

Inhibitions fade as my forest fires rage
Release our destiny locked in celestial cages
To dance with her aura of feminine sage
Across rich valleys my temptation invades
Delicious honey drips like dew from tulips of splendor
Pollinate her garden oasis in tranquility of sweet surrender
Where seedlings of earth and sky float in fertility of divine rivers

Ohi'a Lehua Wild Pua

A painted sky of laughter and sun glance off my eyes of blue imagery.
Reflecting lava shades of opal attract in forces of convergent synergy.
Waves surge... crushing against her South Pacific tenderness of island memory.
Swept across the arc of a rainbow her touch magnetic.
Filling my mind in a torrential rush of life poetic.

A moondance of wildflowers of Ohi'a lehua.
Sultry fragrance of my island pua.
Twinkling stars of cadence shimmer upon cool waterfalls of Wailua
Souls romance... drawn in carriage upon the
Mauka stone of a lost Polynesian night.
Like the brush strokes of pastel impressionism we
intertwine in the violet mist of lunar light.
God's of nature and mythic fortune guide us into new
worlds of passion and flames of delight.

A sensory mirror of flooded reflections float in slack tides of eternity.
Facets of fire burn in deep rooted vines of fantasy and destiny.
We traverse the sea chasing the sun of Winter mystery.
It's warmth upon the heart and evocative beauty Saturate
my thoughts of verse and lucent nobility.
Melts like the pollen of honey bees upon petals of sweet sincerity.

Wet with dew drops of her morning blessing. Darkness of
the universe in depths of onyx slow dissolving.
Spiritual harmony of the soul echo with the gentle foliage of her secret garden.
My sweet wildflower of island fertile seas of rich conception.
Mango trees drape and curtain her nectar of thirst of journey.
Interwoven in a green Naupaka menagerie .
Rhythm of smile with gleam and intimacy.

In the setting sun of liquid honey we write our songs of drifting melody.
Sealed in the bonds of sacred moments of life and breath of energy.

Pageantry

The intimate rush of inviting Asian eyes cascade
Across supple lips of liquid ruby sparkle in breezy trades
Crest of tidal seas ripple in infinite waves of rocky cavalcade
Unveiling life's mystery in poetic masquerade
Hearts beat in harmony in fronds of balmy shade
Loosening inhibitions in shades of gray

Sea foam and wetness caress her breast tone of soft serenity
Beckons my touch of fingertips and masculine affinity

Almond tears of innocence reflect in icy pond of lost pageantry

Her lungs heave with fullness and brevity
Beneath my weight of cosmic gravity
Deep inside her essence of soulful captivity
Searching for truth on distant horizons of earthly tranquility

Her color of rainbow permeates my lost visions
Where the pastel sunset silhouette the sway of palm tree
Illuminate my smile in ocean waves
of passion and creativity

The scent of fragrant perfume lingers in my mind tonight
Alone but felt close her heart of radiant appetite
Come to me in dreams of Aloha to dance under the rich moonlight

Bending curves and hips of feminine delight
Saturates my mind in waterfalls of nature's might
Palms sway in poetry of motion, purity of waves of deep blue sapphire
Waltz upon the sky and sea of songbirds of effortless flight
To find our rhythm of love in the hot Summer night

Parallel Existence

The pathways of the soul weave through dense Naupaka vines of shore lined cliffs
Securely clenched to her sacred land blessed
Bracing against the relentless tides of emerald sea
Firm roots intertwined in a grasp of solidarity
Beneath a Maui sky of blue artistry
Separating earthen elements of solid and liquid density
Each exist in tangent realms of natural simplicity
Poetic verse in harmony of ancient history
Rising from the dark depths of her eyes of coral beauty

I walk the planet of human discovery
Searching for her lyrical breath of angelic perpetuity
Nurturing her seeds and wild flowers of fertility
Embracing the charm of her sojourn mystery
A parallel existence of souls dancing upon distant waves of lunar gravity
Where hearts float like fireflies of bio luminosity
Alluring seas radiate with blue and glistening green
Shining radiantly upon the palms of our lost destiny
Her touch unites... once again to ignite our embers of serendipity

Restless suns gravitate and collide in fires and phosphorus
Heat of impact evaporates the ocean into salty mist upon her supple lips
A collective disarray of iron core meteor
In a fusion of stars of our parallel universe
Lyrical nectar teases the tongue as we converse
Chapters written in a book of love in poetry of verse
Bridging our worlds together in symbiotic unison
We embrace upon the moons of Jupiter and seas of Poseidon
Inebriant fragrance of Plumeria in her hair
Permeates with a aromatic perfume of Aloha in the night air
Spirit of life in the breath of stars beyond compare

Pendulum

Early morning yellow orb glistens upon the opal jewels of her eyes
Translucent in pristine hues across a waning
illuminance of moonbeams hypnotize
Moments lost in virgin seas she sparkles with the allure of a lunar turquoise tide
Salty mist beads like dewdrops upon curves of bronze tone fantasy
Far easterly trades grace the sovereignty of island palms of tranquility

The glow of golden light bends across a pendulum of stars in mirrors of reflection
Warmth of soul and Aloha spirit of attraction
Freezes me in a desire of secret passion
Like Autumn leaves falling in a cold November rain
Pastoral visions of the season upon my glass windowpane
Permeate her lush landscape of earthen terrain

The inviting softness of fingertips reaches deep to massage my soul
To touch the essence of creativity to make my life whole
Like a breath of angelic wind songs
Swaying with the harmony of palm fronds
Musical hearts reverberate with gentile control
Like two silhouettes that always belong
Interwoven with a fabric of celestial bond
Gardens of lilies floating in serene ponds
Moving back and forth with the currents of reflecting pools of intimate charm
Our vines interlace with the embrace of loving arms

Shadows upon the drifting sands of Cameroon
Beneath African skies a rhapsody of white lace consume
Across the hemisphere of fluffy cumulus
A divinity of orchestral beauty invokes a enchanting tune
My muse of mystery of fragrant succulents
Taste of sweet honey and yellow hibiscus
Hearts swimming in a tapestry of magic runes

Phantom

Her phantom aura... poetic embers... a warmth of soul continue to
burn in a phosphorus glow of Aurora Borealis in my heart.
My thirst for her precious ellixor of love falling like succulent
raindrops of island showers upon my dreams in distance apart.
Sweeping across the eons of time takes me away to our
home among the gardens of wet Gardenia.
Her inebriant fragrance of passion adrift in the breeze amongst
the Marigolds of soft melody of ancient Polynesia
Flowing in unison our spirits of golden eagles soar in adulation..
Adrift in my blue eyes of captivating King's chivalry of regal creation.
Emotions awash in a rhythm of musical orchestration.
We meet again my love to embrace the quiet of subtle meditation.
Tying us together in silhouettes of the moonrise our bodies
collide in the sweet elucidation of our intimate liaison.

Her touch of elegance adorns my crown of royal nobility with every breath.
Heaving fullness of breast against me.
Our celestial totems of nativity illuminate the threshold
of our gates of the God's of aristocracy.
Inviting smiles of the Albatross fly above in fluffy cumulus of cotton.
The pathway of our ancestral stars calling us in a lush eroticism.

Consumes us in a insatiable hungering fantasy.
Two lover's of a stormy menagerie echo with the sounds
of thunder and electricity of sensuality.
Flourishing in our eternal lovesongs of life energy.
The world stands still in the fullness of our sultry taste of muscular dexterity.

Lips of ruby obsession choreograph her assault
upon my body in a immortal lucidity.
A jungle of lust in wild animal splendor of seduction.
My caress of manly pleasure undulating against her secret garden oasis.
Radiance in the heat of Summer passion.

Stars explode in the aroma of pure rhythm and cosmic realms
A euphoric romance endures of devotion and tender
memory in visions of fascination.

Poetry of Aloha

The essence of Aloha eyes cast a
glow of richly adorned Lei.
Cut from sacred stones of opal purity.
Inviting as reflecting pools of sea coral.
Immersed in tides of sparkling swirl.
White diamonds of her heart unfurl.
From dreamscapes of lost palm
shadowed sand of Maha'ulepu.
Turquoise waves of infinite
mystery flow from her caress
and crescent winter moon.

Whispering the orchestral
harmony of the universe.
Elegance of nature's artistry.
Her smile saturates the roots
of my soul in wet lucidity.
Fragrance of pua and rainbow prisms
coalesce in stormy serendipity.
Pulsing through my consciousness.
Coursing veins and tremors of arteries.
The illuminance of the stars
vibrant in heavens majesty.

New years begin with wishes
of health and prosperity.
Longing once again for her
taste of wild honey
Innocent touch of supple burgundy.
Like the breath from a soft gentle trade.
Against my skin, emotion
dissolves in amber waves.

Like the vanishing waterfalls
into sleepy Hanalei.
Drifting down lazy rivers
of my ethereal haze.
Her heart beat of Polynesian
rhythm soothes me.
In a perpetual motion of
earthen beauty.

Dance with me beneath the stars
and Na Pali. Waves crest.
Melt into my embrace of
a warm salty mist.
Ignite our fire of Pele passion
with a everlasting kiss.
Hearts and hips collide with the fever
of lava lipstick upon my heaving chest.
Breath of angelic wind
impress upon my neck.
Her island dew beads upon blossoming
petals of my Saharan thirst.
Like a golden nectar... a
sugary voice of serenity.
Calling me across a
hemisphere of gravity.
Compelling us together to share
our cosmos of moonbeams.
Enveloping our souls of
emotion and creativity.
Where notes of musical simplicity
compose the melody of our life energy.

Poet Sunrise•

Her touch is a charm of intimate sensuality I find irresistible as the awakening
island flowers. Indeed, like rays of moonbeams in dreams of lost lovers.
Two hearts of a dynamic chemistry waiting to explode
in my firm grip of words of poetry.
Yes, a fire of passion and rainbows mist... an
intuitive spontaneity when we last kissed.
A garden among the stars is ours to nurture in
fertile seas of lost passion my Venus.
To enchant our souls of celestial charm in each other's pulse of energy between us.
A soothing caress of our virtuous lips... subtle their
touch of luminous shine and consciousness.
Bonds of natural elements burning on the wick of
candles across our divine universe.
A symmetry of sovereign hearts destined to collide in a
brilliance of romance. Forever linked in a intuitive artistry
of emotion of alluring spiritual convergence.
Hearts beat in a tribal song of the night ocean tide of innocence.
Breath and lips to her perfume of wild Hibiscus. A
nectar of wine her temple of heat and fantasy.
Waves of memory and exotic eyes of beauty. Permeates
in the embers of a burning sunrise tapestry.
Painting my Picasso 's in lush brushstrokes of magnetic gravity.
A canvas of colors upon our palates of intimacy.

Polynesian Wind

Adrift on the aroma of radiant hibiscus
Sway of Hula girl beneath island moon crescent
Jet stream of the Pacific above us
Time bends the Milky Way in the distance
Impending waves her divine essence
Lei upon my heart with passionate lace
Eyes of Onyx mistress
Touch of evocative innocence
Like stardust cast from her palm in glittery facets

Island shores fade into the clouds and sea
Lava cliff monuments of Hawaiian mythology
A fondness of Aloha for her romance and intimacy
Polynesian wind carry my sunflower seed

Silver constellations guide across calm tranquility
My eastern light of friendship and Asian fantasy
Radiate and shine your warmth and vivacious energy
Embrace the fate of our soulful seeds

The curvature of heavenly body in hemisphere
Gently my mind grasps her surreal hips of erotic splendor
Lunar lips collide in natural purity and pleasure
Polynesian wind carry me on the wings of feathery dove
Across far horizon her longing caress of euphoric love

The sirens of the sunrise
Wake with morning dew
To walk into her garden of sunflower and Xanadu
Drink from fountains of lilac and cherry blossoms
Like a song sung in perfect tune
Orchestral harmony of the Polynesian wind
Carry my spirit to her presence of song tonight

Postulate of Love ♡ ♡

May your soul find its eternal strength in the wisdom of
a new morning passivity of peaceful life energy.
A passion of sunlight cast in warming tones of love upon your cheek.
Forged in the comfort of vast ocean of stars of the Milky Way galaxy.
A expression of ordained gospel set in the dogmas
of graceful meditative ministry.
Imparting a guidance of navigation of tumultuous reality.
Merging time, space and quantum equations on new plateaus of dimensionality.

Immersing yourself in the aromatic freedom of creations
intimate touch and palatial harmony.

To feed upon the sustenance of emblematic dreams of gypsy perceptibility.
Enlightening the corridors of your footsteps of identity.
A soothing beat of rhythm and torchlight of infantry.
A innocence of the raindrops upon the fallen Autumn leaves.
Walking hand in mine through the orchards of romance and intimacy.

Two beating hearts pulsing in the island breeze of endless love and lucidity.
A ritual of the sermons calling us in a poetic serenity.
The wolfen cries of solidarity to comfort the burning essence of faint memory.
The postulate of existentialism and innate comprehension of spirituality.
Pervades the ink wells of a King's heart and gemstone of nobility.
A vanity of the enigmatic tides of sovereignty.

A harbor of refuge in my arms of orbiting perpetuity.
A gratitude and understanding of our world together
in perplexing smiles of frequency.
A fragrance of midnight eyes of seductive prowess and luminosity.
Enriching the lungs in a deep perfume of lost humanity.
Enticing our verses of lush colorful idolatry.
A river flowing in wet sensuality.
Flourishing in brushstrokes of our emerging Renaissance of Botticelli.

Primal Waves

The eager anticipation of my fingertips await
her sanguine lips of gentle intimacy
Hearts collide in pristine waters of deep blue sea and coral dexterity
Lungs sigh heavy
Inebriant feel of pulsing breast muscle beneath me
Radiant smile and breath of frenetic energy
Her eyes overflowing in cool shadows of willowy palm tree

Melt away inhibitions her gracious smile of femininity
Fate of passion and surreal destiny
Release our hearts of lustful captivity
Charm of Hula dreams of mystery
Impressions upon her soft full lips
Like the warmth of oil massaged across curves and hips
Inviting my caress of masculine serenity

Her embrace of romance dissolves the separation and pain
Her kiss lingers of lost lovers in island rain
Primal attraction of energies flowing through arteries and left side brain
Destined to find each other's pulse and sandy footsteps
Two souls walk along a beach of celestial charm and eloquence
The spirit of Aloha imparts blessings and gifts

Heartbeats skip as a simple smile lifts
To touch my life of gray with colorful riffs
Her presence inside illuminates like burning torches in mythic journey
The weight of passion in seismic gravity
I will carry in soulful essence of perpetuity
Long distance love will only fade so we must find a way
A hui hou my island wahini in the fragrant sunrise of a new earthly day

Purity

A purity of island wind sings in the ardent tropic air of night
Rustling green palm fronds sway in waves of diligent delight
Ocean tides crash upon her labyrinth cliffs with laboring thundering might
A soothing harmonic energy
Strumming the orchestral chords of my vagrant mortality

Nature's artistry speaks in a universal language of synergy
To those who listen and let go the facades of mankind's ambiguity
Absorbing like the warmth of Tahitian trades embrace the heart
Saturating dreams of lost romance and destiny
Impermanence of island sands dissolving into seas of distant memory
Her Polynesian smile languishes in deep fathoms of eager soulful discovery

A spirit of the wind transcends and withers the rigid corals of callous disparity
To expose life's basic truths with gritty honesty
Illuminating like the sunrise on a new horizon imparts
Across the hemisphere of gravity and starry fountains
We find our solace among the elements of earthly realm
To begin each day anew again

A cleansing and purity of compassion
Touches the surface of romanticism
Clears the dark skies of my disillusion
Flesh and bone becomes ash in fires stoked in mother nature's affection
Lunar crescent winds of moonshine inebriate with sweet confection
Light the pathways of heavens majesty and creationism
In the pureness of a night breeze of aromatic vision

Rainbow Soul

A refraction of light of spiritual shrine
casts its blessing upon the palm
Shine down from heavenly
skies in hues of artful song
Earthly passion of green flora
and waves of blue beyond

Intimate smile... eyes of nature's purity
reflect the soul of child's innocence

Leaping across hemisphere
and shifting tides and sun
Raindrops of her solemn footsteps
fall...soft tears against the subtle
fabric of a mother's weeping heart
Melancholy stillness of color...
impressionist tones of the frozen
river palate of Renoir
Chasing her rainbow soul
of passion and spark

Ivory keys of pearl gates open and
fade like stars guiding the Albatross
A melody of psalm, devotion
of faith in religious witness
Showering stardust in a daughter's
grace of innocent love
Wrapped in God's Kingdom
of infinite caress

Myriads of luminosity and
lucid musical tone
Alluring, sifting granules lulls the
heart beat of emotion cast against
life's hourglass of white sandstone
Soaring in a majesty of
mystique in faceted haze

Iridescent spectrum of
prayerful thoughts convey
Melt like snowflakes into maternal
clouds of stormy grey
To lift her pulse of heart on a new day

A mother's touch to calm
the spirit of humanity
A cohesiveness of inner consciousness
and natural beauty
Filters like dappled sunlight through
trees of inherent serendipity
Painting the imagination of
hope and individuality
Permeating her slumbering
consciousness
In a divinity of spirit of
Christian philosophy

Primary colors of the universe
Backlit with essence of vanilla sky
Evocative presence of
wavelengths in her eyes
Enchanting treasures await
to enrich a future bride
Captivating like the warmth
of July fireflies
A hue of coral reefs glistening in saltiness
Inviting with a warmth of
pearls of pure white
Moist petals of flowers radiate
with the gentle fragrance of life
Birds of Paradise wafting in
soft lunar crescent tide
Chasing her rainbow of soul on
airwaves and divinity of sunlight

Restless Hearts ♡ ♡

Her heart beats in restless tides of passionate convergence.
Swirling in a dervish of raven hair and succulent Hibiscus.
Palpitating upon the palms of my desolate wilderness.
Fragrance of Lilac and lips of peppermint caress.

Mystic waves; my muse of the sea.

Rush upon sandy shores of island fantasy.
Sing me your melody of intimate odyssey.
Rage against my towering cliffs.
Relentless upon my pulse of consciousness.
Yearning in ocean fathoms, her touch deft and ubiquitous.

Incessantly burning in a cauldron of complexity.
One spark ignites her volcanic flow of energy.
Heat of a thousand suns to greet me.
Eruptions of thundering lava storms shake me.
Surging into seas of her Polynesian mystery.
Create our earthly seeds of memory.
Restless heart of a distant rose dance upon white washed stars of the galaxy.
Blossoming with the eternal light of emotion and destiny.

Enveloped in a embrace of sensuality and romance from my lady of dreams.
Her restless heart beats implicitly for my touch along moonlit streams.
Her perfume lingers and saturates my heat of flesh.
A kiss of celestial beauty with moondust of soulfulness.
Shower me in your haven of stars eternally.
Glittery facets of charm and serenity .
Drink in her love songs shining radiantly.
Like the morning dew of Aloha spirituality.

Royal Blue

Thoughts wander in tidal footsteps of supple white sands of resolve.
Beneath the sway of tradewinds admist the rustle of night palm.
Listening to the music of her heart song calling across her ocean of calm.
A lyrical melody of liquid soul summoned to destiny.

Guided by constellations of starlit eternity.
Lost in a fragrance of inebriant royalty.
Drifting in the coconut salty breeze.
A soothing harmonic complexity.
Strumming my chords with her intimate symphony.
Her subtle waves dance over me in lunar gravity.

Sifting granules of the hour glass curves pour slowly but surely.
The miracle of life and intimacy of two souls resolve in orbits of acendency.
As the planets revolve in the tapestry of heavenly body of the Milky Way galaxy.
Our spirits soar into the fading orange orb and royal blue sea of melody.

The ancestral love we cherish and hold dearly.
Beyond sacred totems of native song and theory.
Philosophies written in the stars above will forever shine.
Coelescing elements of the universe mold the world of intrinsic design.
Shaping visions of tomorrow in the jewels of her mystic onyx eyes.
In the beat of two hearts of kind and cognitive mind.
We share the blessing of Aloha and reverence of the aura of the divine.

Scarlet Heart

She is the poetry of my heart
Radiant as the sun kissed oceans of blue in my world apart
A birth of new song in a melody of island meadowlark

Her silhouette sways with lazy palm in my eyes... star struck
Lips of ruby with a touch of scarlet
Cushioned by gentle trades drifting through my shadow of watery dark
Engraving my imagination in a sculptured work of Italian art

The fathoms of her seas invoke my verses of spirit and intimacy
To grace my presence in a tsunami of strength and subtle creativity
Freedom of the Makai blesses humanity with her waves of tidal fertility
Sturdy roots intertwine our songs in lyrical gardens of undersea odyssey
Like a fabled tapestry of a lover's menagerie
Swimming in her whisper of raging fantasy

Pulsing vibrations and surging palpitations
Dance like sonic tones of infinite sensation
Permeate my heart of scarlet in seductive libations
A symphony of seismic proportions
Wells in my soul with a effervescent sanguine absorption
Lost in her essence of fragrant consumption
Saturates my flesh in a coolness of aloe lotion from my burning passion

Lipstick dreams of feathery softness of Red Cardinal
Eclipse the elements of the heavens and earthly realms
To immerse myself in her Windsong of Mozart's
tympanic world
Graceful wings conducting a beauty of composition unfurl in a purity of pearls
Inter woven in our hearts of scarlet and spiritual harmony
A taste of romance beneath our galaxy
A sweet dessert of erotic flavor and delicious inspiration of poetry

Secret Garden

An earthly truth of serene emotion guides the heart of longing fire.
Tangled knots of raging expression of caged desire.
Surging in the strength of trade winds sifting in
my thoughts below blue Hale heavens.
A smile of enchantment exquisite with eyes of glossy onyx.
Dissolves into my lips her savory spice of coconut... most poetic and eclectic.

Beneath her waves run deep in virtue of feminine soul.
Echoeing across the sandy dunes and sacred Naupaka voices sustain.
Off the cliffs of NaPali her infinite song of nature's sernade.
She comes to me in a mystery of haze and comfort
to my Hawaiian spiritual crusade.
Malleable my mind in sensory deluge of the sunset
whispering her name as warm thoughts pervade.

Souls woven into the fabric of time find sustenance upon the coral edifices made.
Inoculate the harsh realities of our temporal mortal waves.
Etched upon our totems of life and breath of lung we find solemnity.
Pulsing heartbeat and blood flows between our desires and destiny.
Rays glisten upon her distant isle of grace in fading orange and red burgundy.
A hui hou beyond the ocean mist our souls meet in subtle unity.
Footprints emboldened upon the sands of metaphor and memory.
Two lover's resonate with a touch of intimate discovery.
Emotions emblazoned in the heat of Polynesian deities.
Her spirit of Pele burns with savage wisdom and veracity.

Like DNA flowing in worldly veins of purity and fantasy.
A freedom of Aloha upon her secret gardens of majesty.
Hearts blending in lunar tides of the moon of temple ministry.
A melody upon my flesh and inner consciousness.
Strum my chords of orchestral movement of the universe.
Inextricably sewn through time and season.
Touch of fate our time together reason.
Fortuitous rhyme and blessing upon our spirits of invitation.
We revel upon the verses of seclusive archeology.
Forever revolving in celestial gravity our hearts of natural beauty.

Shakespeare's Envy

I miss my island flower of Juniper
Like the suave touch of my fabled Juliette
A poem of serene spirit invoking my passion and lyric.
Pulse fluttering... aching cauldrons burn within our raging heart.
A intoxicating flavor of soul tantalizing her hungry palate of colorful art
A invisible easterly wind caressing her flesh across oceans afar.

We drink from the fountain of euphoria
Whispering through the orchards of Plumeria
Her smile glowing... hair flowing as our touch imparts.
Melodies of Jupiter with a lullaby of stars.
Eyes of turquoise dissolve into a mythic ascension of Venus and Mars.
Souls embrace the eternal spark.
An oasis of deliverance from our shadows apart.

Our words dance in a literary romance.
As the planets interlope in glimmering distance.
Moonflowers blossom with a effervescent charm and fragrance.
Reflections in mirrors of watery memory.
Idyllic verses in undersea gardens of a dolphins smile of intimacy.
To enscribe our verses of Shakespeare's envy
Upon the coral edifices of emotion and sculptured identity.
Aloft in a tapestry of Angelic voices of harmony.

The insurgency of her tides of liquidity.
Move my mind in a revolving eccentricity.
A potion of graceful hospitality.
To taste her salty mist of sacred pageantry.
Hemlock of the galaxy and fires of Aphrodite.
Surrendering to our bonds of destiny.
We waltz among the raindrops of a summer rain.
Where souls rejoice in the purity of poetic thoughts sustained.
In the melancholy stillness of island teardrops of heartfelt pain.

Silver Pearl

Her warm embrace of eternal soul melts my frosty
atmosphere with a scent of lily and lilac
Wafting into my depth of consciousness with the warm trades of the Kona breeze
Subtle grace of shady palms invites the stars to shine in melodic psalm
Songs of radiance, a tranquil calm
Pastel eyes of almond, hair draped long
Like the brush strokes of Salvador Dali across the infinite terrain of my soul
Invitingly surrealistic

Permanent waves of passion invoke a journey
beholden to the paths of flaming comets
Across dark sky we ignite and paint the heavens... her touch angelic.
Phosphorus and enigmatic
Monarchs dance with passion.. soft and romantic
A Journey of Soul enchanting and eclectic

The wisdom of the divine will always shine bright
Upon my shy eyes of blue and white
Unravel my heart of tangled knots
Her silver of pearl discovery within my thoughts
Where natural light bends into myriads of rainbows sought
Reflecting in tide pools of my internal yearning beating pulse hard fought

We share a bond of fateful attraction captivatingly intrinsic
In nature's wake submerged under seas of lush gardens... charismatic
Bonds of energy soothing and rhythmic
Internal meanderings of the soul
Inebriant and poetic
Teach the lessons of life of Shaman philosophic
Harmony of nature and humanity unveils the mystery and purpose
of our existence in the quintessential stars of her divine spirit

Song of Lauoho

Hearts of thunder echo like the falls of Waipo'o surging with mountain rain.
Opaque skies harken with the rushing sound of nature's serenade.
Flowing like blood through thick rivers of coarsing vein.
The courtship of the Albatross embues the mystery
of her love song of Lauoho Lane.
Emotions fostered in bituminous eyes of friendship... blossoming
like Spring Plumeria and flowering Plantain.
Where comets of Geminid rise in memory and the
harmony of my Aloha spirit remain.
A storied tapestry of the shadows of soul chasing the sunset of infinite domain.
Lost in waves of distant energy I can't explain.
Immersed in the lavishing touch of enchanting discovery unable to contain.
Nourishing my world of hunger with a kiss of celestial champagne.
Ravishing wild instincts of her hypnotic trance of imprisoning opalescent chains.
I lay upon her warm quilt of Hawaiian majesty.
A swirling gravity of the cosmos guides my Queen of longing intimacy.
A dreamy sensual inception of our lives of incantation and reflection.
Composing the orchestral movement of indelible stars of collision.
Magnetic her poetic resonance of feminine persuasion.
Lips meet in a rogueness of sweet seduction.
Bodies embrace in the bonds of her sacred garden.
Eternal souls of natural light bend into prisms of emboldened rainbow.
Basking in the tranquility of scented grove of Coconut and Mango.
Relishing moments beneath a wintry lunar glow.
Where chords of magical notes blend as verse and song of my lady of Lauoho.
Forever inspired with the soft melody of my island ku'uipo.
Interwoven in the violet seas of romance beyond the stars of Kalaheo.

Spring Eternal

Earthly realms of the season.
Beneath soft melodies of the moon flowers in rhyme and sage reason.
Blossom in the companionship of daffodils of early Spring.

Bent towards the warm horizon of sun slipping beyond as Dolphin's sing
A freedom of spirit of Monarch butterfly.
Like a fluttering heart on the wind of time flies by.
Her eyes of opal invite and simply mystify.
Dressed elegantly in the starch of white cumulus
and golden essence of a sapphire sky.

Our life minerals of the universe forged in the
cauldrons of nature's riotous mastery.
Bodies pump with blood and consciousness of the soul of eternity.
Guide us to each other's touch upon lunar ships of fruitful intimacy.
Searching for her treasures of supple petals of feminine majesty.
A gravity of storm laden seas consume me with intensity.

Effortlessly drawn like pollen to the honey bee.
Our wild hunger for sugary confection of nectarine.
Our celestial embrace of primordial fate.
Cements two hearts in the palate of thirst of a lost soulmate.
Cosmic destiny linked in the surging waves of our arterial pulse rate.
A musical rhythm that blends together with a
radiance of the ethereal peacocks feather.

Islands in the sun kissed stone of dawns arrival.
Embolden our path among the gardens of secret passion and seeds of survival.
We share the blessing of fortune's wheel of deep
emotions and thoughts existential.
A taste upon our lips that springs eternal.
Walking in each other's sandy imprints.
Our journey pervades the tides of liquidity and lost romance.
Drifting in subtle fragrance to entice a mythic Knights heart to
his Queen's alluring spell of enchantment and reverence.

Star of Kalaheo

Intrepid stars of Kalaheo shine upon her heart in slumbering
trek across the darkness of Polynesian skies.
My shadows slip away into the mist of Nigerian sea of lost romance.
Fleeting in thoughts that remain.
Like rainbows of the summer rain.
Permeate the essence of lucidity of my inner terrain.
In wishing wells of the soul.
Dreams dissolve into a mythic reign.
Beckon my presence upon her longing kiss of celestial champagne.
Eternal script of floating bottles through time. Messages beyond
horizons bobbing in tidal moonshine. A lyrical purity rushes through
lungs inebriant in sensual odyssey of cosmic rays of light.
Lanterns of the fireflies to guide thoughts in languishing reservoirs. Illuminate
her vision to my wayward shores. Walk with me through intimate gardens
of oasis.. sculpted from the divine in shifting sands of desert contours.
The current of deep oceans bridge our world together.
Surging tides of white wash upon her bronze tone flesh and auburn hair.
A smile of enchantment. Exquisite charm, debonair. Drip like vines
of honeysuckle upon fullness of lips and eyes of darkness.
Adrift on seas of celestial Venus.
Spirits meet in thickening atmosphere.
Passions unite soulmates to embrace our beat of consciousness of the universe.
Create the nebulous of attraction and flirtatious conception.
To plant our fertile seeds in earthly affection. Evocative
touch of a Queen's alluring presence.
Grace of swans caress. Compassion and finesse. We float with
the butterflies on the flowering wind of Lauoho.
Beneath our star of Kalaheo.

Moon Blonde

A summer blonde moon of July arches across ripe papaya fields of festive Luau
Friendly lunar light bends and curves with leeward
trades brushing raised eyebrow
Shades of verdant land.. plush like tropic gardens of Kalalau
Streams of golden Maui flow from mountains in the Valley of Iao
Nature's blessing will always endow

A orchard blossoms with blending symphony and arrangement
To dissolve the hardship of life's disillusionment
A lingering fragrance of orchid remembrance
Inertia of wandering footsteps in ancient gardens of Sumeria
Waltz in poetic cadence of a aromatic night of euphoria

Clandestine candles burn bright as we meet this warm July night
Smiles radiate Aloha in waves of enchanting delight
Blonde and gold tassels upon bronze tone flesh and eyes
Shoulder my depth of conscience and attraction in thematic rhymes
Summer moon blonde... dance upon forests of mangoes and limes
Lunar rays of silk dapple between our eager fingertips
Icy comets melt upon thy heart in island ruby lips
A swans fullness of grace upon pleasures of hula hips
Exquisite taste.. sweet dreams of innocence
The galaxy of humanity lives beyond earthly seed
Beyond untouched rings of Saturn and Kauaian air we breathe
The pearls of the sea are our universe to discover intuitively
To write the story of poetic fate and intimacy

Summer Solstice

Whispering Hawaiian moon lay in stillness of the warm summer night.
Perched upon meadows of amber and dew.
Palm shaded statues of rhythm dancing in their labyrinth of gold crescent blue.
A perfume of passion gravitates with the lunar draft of soft summer wind.
Across inhalant breath and lung her musings of harmonic tune.
Casting spells of young lover's in the shadow of blonde strands consume.

Desire compels our yearning of dreams come true.
A natural attraction of fateful stars aloft.
Melodic kiss of wet cherry blossom in rain so soft.
Against silky flesh pulse beat, frenetic in motion
Pageantry of white Plumeria.
Lay upon her bronze tone in ocean moons of night.

Thoughts disappear like distant sun of galaxies, longing kiss of Eden's caress.
Exotic flavor, Asian fruits tantalize her thirsty lips of eagerness.
Meteoric power fuels our fire.
Burning hearts collide in fervor of lunatic tide.

Surging in brevity of luminate emotion euphoric.
Souls combine in misty fables of the south Pacific.
Forever intertwined in impressionistic images of the artistic.
Dance upon the clouds with each other's essence.
Blessed by cherubs of passion and flirty elegance.
Sipping upon julips and cool mint.
Unveils the mystery of precocious elements.
In deep almond eyes of elation and exuberance.

Ionian Wave

Whispering Ionian waves of starlight possess her
sanguine heart in heat of the Oahu night
Perched upon dreamy sands of amber and dew kissed palms she takes my hand
Sailboats float in picturesque serenity moored in
their labyrinth of gold crescent moonlight
A perfume of passion gravitates off her flesh of lunar lit tan
Across inhalant breath and lung intimate musings of harmonic tune
Casting spells of young lover's in the touch of my
fingertips as her gypsy laden strands consume

A compelling wave of Summer love stokes the
yearning fire in my souls surge of emotion
An attraction of our burning fateful stars aloft
Melodic kiss of wet cherry blossom gentle and soft
Against my pulse of heart beat, frenetic in motion
Exotic pageantry of white virgin Plumeria
Lay upon my bronze chivalry of Polynesia in seductive sounds of the night ocean

Thoughts disappear like distant sun of galaxies, a
longing kiss of Eden's truth and goodness
Exotic flavor, Hula girl hips tantalize, thirsty lips of eagerness
Meteoric power on the wings of Icarus
Heartbeats rampant in a fervor of a crazed lunatic
Surging in brevity of the luminate moon euphoric
Souls collide in misty fables of a King and Queen's love story
Forever intertwined in impressionistic images of virtuosity
Dance upon the clouds with each others essence
Blessed by cherubs of passion and flirty elegance
Sipping upon julips and cool mint
Unveils the mystery of bonds of precious elements

In deep blue facets her eyes of elation and exuberance

Sweet Surrender 🙏💙

Her wet canvas of painted provocation drips with colors of lusty inspiration.
Our souls embrace in our minds and hearts of an
inhalant breath of our surreptitious passion.
My wayward soul drifts with a intimate aroma of her perfumed
laced femininity saturating my night wind aura of seclusion.
Like a salty breeze flowing from the waters of Waikiki Bay
calling my name in a sirens song of love and seduction.
I surrender to her essence of womanly charm and eloquence of soulful intuition
Glisten in my eyes of blue subterranean in oceans of introspection

The abstinence of elusive sensual indulgence resolves in a
dream fantasy of unspoken liturgy of eroticism
A sensory deprivation of romantic waves of tender disposition
command our weaponry of salacious fanaticism
My warriors battle cry with the wolf assault the
supple innocence of your alabaster flesh
Devouring every kiss in my eyes of blue caress
Drinking in the distilled flavor of untamed spirit of romance

Our bonds grow with the strength of rooted vines of Naupaka
and soar with the Albatross of destined flight
Absorbing the nutrients of life and sustenance to ripen
our fruits of passion in rays of island sunlight
Enriching our palates of intimate fire of the oceans of embrace we
stoke the embers of the flames of our prosperity of future life

Awash in the tails of comets we possess a natural exotic beauty
Her touch and unity of our souls of sublimation delight
Embryonic flow of discovery fills the heart with a birth of evocative sight
Vibrant as sturdy Live Oaks of Spanish moss draped in sultry moonlight
Breathing our oxygen of luminous fragrance of vibe
Surrendering our hearts to each other in ethereal emotions of eternal tide

Tribal Love ♡ ♡

My mind echoes upon the safe harbor of intimate solidarity of perception.
Words of love and poetry of late night liason.
Evocative pleasure and songs of dedication.
Eyes precipitant with the sweet caress of feminine surrealism.
Eternal flames of devotion.

Floating on her effervescent charm of seduction.
Inviting touch of living energy. Soulful wonder
dancing through waves of my emotion.
Intersecting the virtuous path we travel in fervent collision.

Meteoric principles... the matter of celestial origin.
Primordial elements of pure magnetic attraction.

Bonding inseparable wavelengths of interactive sunlight.
Oceans of blue, earthly domain in a divine pulse of life.
A feverish passion exudes from my yearning heart to melt in her arms tonight.

Billowing sails upon our ship of honeymoon.
Silhouettes backlit in a cavalcade of stars of Orion
Adrift in adventure of newlyweds in latent aromatic spice.
Conquering the universe of our souls of celestial paradise.
Her helm upon my ship to guide us across the onyx of night.
With a warmth of lush vision of Karma of life.

In the liturgy of poetic bonds...
Seeds take root deep... womb of fertile seas of ocean.
Bridal passion... grooming intimacy of conception
Inextricably sewn through a fabric of time and self compulsion.
Tribal love of unity and solemnity of lovers.
Matrimonial seduction.
Polynesian winds of illusive beauty.
Sensual sands of intuition.
Transcendent in hearts and minds of ancestral perpetuity.
Spirit animals of our souls take flight
Mantra of freedom and creative light

Turquoise River ◈

Blue skies of luminance in heavenly dance
Lift the passion of human spirit and romance
Shades of native turquoise rivers appear and disappear
Clouds of cirrus drift across in wispy white strands of stratosphere
A transcending peace between man and immortal ascension
Earthly mountain breathes with lapping dark depth of ocean

High above in ethereal glow
Flowers beckon the sun to walk her worldly garden sewn
Where butterfly wings float on updrafts of the Tahiti songbirds
Pastel melody of nature interwoven with the fabric of time
Finite elements of hydrogen and oxygen rhyme
Miracle of magic and life design

Lazy streams of music and sensuous sunbeams
Lay upon my heart of peace pulsing in rhythmic scenes
Absorbing her precious energy
Bombarding photons of mysterious mastery
Infinite in cosmic ray my hemisphere of blue dissolves into eyes of ardent green
Unending scriptures of the universe
Lie deep within sand script of ancient poetic verse

Hearts of humanity bend under pressure of viral strain
In a cold darkness of early Spring rain
Wander the skies of turquoise river
Shake the icy tentacles of jagged slivers
Immerse the soul in translucent blue waters
Revelations of spirit rise on the wings of Albatross
Upon the zephyrs of the Easter tide
Gracious her immaculate touch
Where heaven and earth collide
In faith, heart, and breath of sea subside

Ubiquity ♡ ♡ 🙏

The ubiquitous aura of her morning lips resonate from
last night's sea of dreams of Shaman spiritualist
Like the arrows of a cherubs quiver penetrating my vibrance of breathing chest
The infinite rising crest of golden orb with a lasting
warmth upon my trembling flesh

In melodic verses of her sacred caress my beat of heart rests
A rhythm of love in a ballad of smooth finesse
Inspirational wishes of sweet seductiveness
Lucidity of our stars of passion... endearing and effortless

Emanating skies of blue sparkle in her eyes above tides of Pacific
Languish in my pulse of blood and consciousness
She lights up my emotions of the universe
A sensory perception of pure ectasy and sultriness

The elation of my hunger to feel her strokes of Rembrandt's brush
A Renaissance of divinity of surging longingness
In my embrace of sentiment she invokes a quiet storm of tenderness
Waves upon the thirst of my wanton sensuality of lust

Dance of Hula charm in the aromatic perfume of passionate romance
Futility of my heart's resistance
Like the sonnet of Neruda in my morning mist
She intertwines with the heavens of intimate dominance
To unite our lives of inner child playgrounds of rebirth

A belonging in facets of glittering seeds of stardust
Flowing in poetic streams of a reality of internal softness
Like two doves of feathery softness
Our Love will endure in a immortal reign of celestial nest
Enchanting treasures of her nubile touch of elegance 🎸

Under Her Sea

Wild instincts unleash themselves in a tsunami of strength and power
Inevitable revival of nectar of Spring flowers
A desire of hearts turn reality of fantasy Soulmates of spiritual
and earthly destiny Drinking from the stars of golden honey

Beat of heart worship her temple of intimate dominance
Dancing on the sands of fragrant romance
Planting seeds deep inside her fertility of soul
Like the winter snowstorms of white gold
Savoring fruits of our passion in lucid dreams

Hearts coalescing in a nebulous of love serene
Pulsing in rhythm to a purity so clean
Where passionate voices meet in clear running streams
Lay your infinite grace of power and domain
In oceanic depths... a serenity of Aloha refrain

Let me be your sea of calm along a sanctuary of twin palm
Swaying in unison
Flowing in the softness of leeward wind.
Rooted forever in the emotion of tides
Souls washed in a purity of lighted signs
Delicate balance of yin and yang
In a flavor of fresh lemon meringue
Whipped into a frenzy of afternoon appetite
Wild seduction of savory feminine delight

Renaissance of sovereign King and Queen
A feast upon the heart of celestial origin supreme
Swimming in fathoms of infinite seas
Alive with dolphins yearning intimacy
I long for my island flower of sweet sincerity

Wild Instinct ♡ ♡

My heart wanders in her whispering fables of passion
Awaking to a suns crown of a Dionysis creation
Languishing tides awash in a dream... A Saharan desert of melody
Spiritual harmony of earth and seven sea
Fluid motion of hemisphere and fantasy
Dripping heart of desert thirst reign upon my flesh of muscle bead
Nurturing my intimate oasis of internal seed.
Charming night shower of the Pleiades flash... scorching of seductive intrigue

Celestial Gemini waterfalls pour into deep shades of reflecting pools
A poetic stardust of laws magnetic
Saturate the earthen beauty of my life specific
Wild instinct of our romantic verses prolific
Coalescing elements soar and uplift into her skies of blue mystic
Across a pastel of painted native skies natives
speak in sacred canyon hieroglyphic
Introspective thought weights my mind of ancestral perception
Carved in solidarity of heartfelt etchings... engraved
upon my cliffs of strata invocation

Tribal hearts beat as one in each other's pulse of bloodline
Engaged in a evocative nuance of the Maui sunrise
Lips of Polynesian gypsy spirit hypnotize
Bodies intertwine in a choreography of fire and flames
Vortices of the soul struggle in chains of addiction...
dry as arid lands of vast emotion
A sensory mirror of flooded reflection
Faceted glimmer of rhythmic adoration
Rises in warm hues of selfless invitation
Adrift on her waves of eternal sublimation
Sun and shadow of her eyes of natural selection

Wishing Wells of Aloha 👍

Crushing torrent of Wailua falls reverberate
Infiltrate my heart of fatal attraction
Worlds of different beats
Colliding stars of gravitation
Pulse in rhythm of Gemini in the night solar wind

A familiar fabric of memory
Echoes her misty melody
Youthful fragrance of Plumeria
Wandering footsteps in islands of Polynesia
Seedlings blossom then fade in pastel shades of Gardenia

Adventurous heart dance with vitality
Caressing touch like the waves upon the sands of distant Maha'ulepu
A tender kiss upon resting eyes under lunar crescent moon
Swimming in wishing wells of soft lullaby tune

Breath of gentle spirit
Sing me her island song
Against my beating chest
Verses depth of tranquil inner conscious
Where souls swim in the wishing wells of fate and prophecy
Submersed in poetic lyrics of tapestry
Nature's blessing of intimate artistry

🎸